ARE MEN REALLY WOMEN WITH PENISES?

Eric B. Gibson

Smashwords Edition

Are Men Really Woman with Penises? / Eric B. Gibson First Edition

ISBN 978-1-688975-06-4

CONTENTS

DEDICATION

I would like to express my gratitude to the many people who saw me through in my completion of this book. To all those who freely shared their wisdom and understanding, provided support, talked things over freely, read, wrote, offered comments, allowed me to quote their remarks, and assisted in the editing, proofreading, and design. I would especially like to thank my sex-education teacher, Professor Ulla Anderson, for contributing additional material, research, and assistance with the writing of this book.

Eric B. Gibson

"People were hermaphrodites until God split them in two, and now all the halves wander the world over seeking one another. Love is the longing for the half of ourselves we have lost."

Plato

INTRODUCTION

"Are men really women with penises?" After considering this investigative report, I invite you to draw your own conclusion. My job here is simply to furnish you with the evidence and facts necessary for you to make an intelligent decision. This report offers a plausible, alternate theory of the origins of humanity. We've sought to answer the riddle that great thinkers and philosophers have pondered for many generations: From what source did humanity emerge? Was it conceived male out of female or female out of male?

The prevailing idea of a female creation from a male origin is predicated upon the foundation that God created man first (out of clay), and that woman was subsequently created from a man's body, specifically his rib. For as long as anyone can remember, we have been asked to entertain this allegory; Adam, then Eve. However, we are asking you, with an open mind, to consider an alternate theory, "what if just the opposite were true? What if we discovered that women existed on the earth before a man had even graced the soil we stand on today?

As it turns out, our research justifies this hypothesis. The X chromosome, possessed by what we call the feminine species, had existed for at least 65,000 years before the arrival of the Y chromosome (characterized as the male chromosome). The Y chromosome may be the X chromosome with a missing branch (XY). Additionally, citing the genetic timeline, the evidence is irrefutable: All men have within every cell of their bodies the mitochondria of their mothers. This is the source of their genetic makeup. This genetic chain can be traced back to a single female who lived about 200,000 years ago. "Mitochondrial Eve" carried the potential for male and female reproduction.

It is a fact; man is the evolutionary consequence of a feminine being. He is the bone of her bone and flesh of her flesh. Gender roles and subsequent classification arose with the emergence of a male dominant society. Male and female classifications are relatively standardized today because this is what the early fathers of science decided long ago. If you have a penis, you are a boy, and a vagina, you are a girl. However, many people go their whole life questioning their own sexuality, not knowing that they have hidden within their bodies a full or partial set of reproductive organs corresponding to the opposite sex.

Before sexual identification became normalized, humans were essentially gender neutral. Nature presented a comprehensive range of sex types; but men, who arose from women drew the boundaries of man and woman. The age of male domination appeared fairly recently in human history, coinciding with the systematic undoing of Matriarch authority. Our ancestors lived as nomadic hunters, gatherers, and fishers for over 99 percent of human history. Beginning around 10,000 years ago, during the Paleolithic era, we begin to see a change; humans began staying in one place, sedentary, growing crops, and raising domesticated animals.

Farming not only brought changes to the way we obtained food, but it also altered social relations. The agricultural revolution brought competition for land. From this competition arose the notion of male domination, slavery and subsequently war. If we are to understand violence and oppression in our culture today, we must revisit Genesis and reexamine our origins. The vast web of life must follow a logical algorithm. Man cannot exist be- fore the woman that he emerged from. Can a creation ever precede the materials that compose its being? Can an afterglow ever precede its glow? Can an echo exist before the sound that reverberated it into existence? It's impossible. Man has claimed he existed before the mother of all creation who formed him in her womb, bone of her bone and flesh of her flesh. The genetic timeline, as recorded, is irrefutable.

This report offers humanity a clearer understanding of man's genesis, because the story we were given simply does not add up. As recent as a thousand years ago the word "man," translated in German included both man and woman, male and female; it simply meant "human being," void of sexual distinction. It was not until man exalted himself as lord and master of the planet, that the social identity of man and woman were branded upon the human species. Man made himself the ruler of this new world. The ancients from the beginning of civilization neither had a concept of gender or rulership. The timeline for the appearance of sexual identification is important, for it coincides with the biblical timeline of man's fall from grace.

About six thousand years ago the lives of our ancestors began to dramatically shift; an organized campaign swept the earth, under the authority of religion. Acting upon religious decree, the goal of man was clear, "be fruitful and become many, fill the earth and subdue it, and have in subjection the fish of the sea and the flying creatures of the heavens and every living creature that is moving on the earth." Continent by continent, men took upon themselves a responsibility and position no human had ever occupied before, since the conception of the world, and that is dominion by force. The period that man seized authority over the earth coincides with what many scholars refer to as "the fall of humanity," a period of unparalleled violence, chaos and confusion.

Food shortages, global warming, water contamination, etc., to name a few, are all global issues that developed under patriarchal domination. Emergence of new genetic findings indicate that Man was not the first-born of creation and that he indeed emerged from the woman. This leaves us many questions: Who is man? Where did he come from and does he have the legal right and intuitive wisdom to rule the planet? Assigning answers to these questions is what this book seeks to accomplish.

Chapter One:
A TIME WHEN WOMEN RULED

THE BOLD HYPOTHESIS, "Are Men Really Women with Penises" is an intellectual shock to most readers. The evidence presented within these pages permits the reader to entertain another possibility; an alternative to the story that we have been given. Namely, that man was created in God's image, and the woman was created from man, thus assuring him the right to rule as the firstborn. At the heart of this hypothesis is the revolutionary idea that woman like beings came into existence many thousands of years before man, and that man evolved from these feminine beings.

The implications of this emerging scientific paradigm extend into virtually every aspect of our life. Assuming, for a moment, that women did originate before man, the question becomes: "would the world be a safer, more secure environment if it was ruled from a feminine perspective?" Unfortunately, we can only speculate because the fact of the matter is that the world, for the past six thousand years, has been ruled by men. Nonetheless, anyone given an honest appraisal of history and its neverending saga of endless wars and domination would have to admit that man has failed to bring about the basic desires of the pure hearts to live without conflict. How long does a failed way of life continue before a better way of life is accepted?

This book also offers a plausible explanation for the thousands of years of failure under male domination. Simply put, what if it's just not in the cards for a man to rule? Certainly, if man was meant to rule the planet then his rule would have been more successful. Men may serve better in other capacities, but when it comes to leadership, he has failed miserably. Which begs the question was man ever supposed to be the dominant species over every other species on the earth in the first place? This question was answered thousands of years ago in the Bibles' Book of Jeremiah, which reads: "O LORD, I know that the way of man is not in himself: it is not in man who walks to direct his own steps." If the claims of the Bibles' writer are true, man cannot, and should not, even so much as govern himself. He is in need of guidance. Without a doubt, man has had a hard life over the millennia. He too is a victim of his own violence. A changing of the guards from masculine domination to feminine rule could be a blessing in disguise to men all over the world. I say this with great confidence because this is the way it was for men in the beginning. The species called "man" was literally nurtured into existence by a loving tribe of Matriarch mothers.

To understand man's true origin, our minds must be open to new truths. While studying about the age of the Matriarch, it is imperative that we put aside prejudice and gender bias. Be prepared to consider this material with a fresh set of eyes. Let the investigation lead you and be willing to travel beyond the scope of conventional wisdom, outside of the labyrinth of our modern day thought process. We are being introduced to a vastly different world than the one we were born into, the age of matriarch predates the age of self (ego) by thousands of years, yet the age of ego is what we were all born into.

Self-awareness arrived about six thousand years ago with the birth of consciousness (the ability to recognize oneself as an individual separate from both the environment and other individuals). With no mirrored presence, the ancient forerunners of our world had no perception of self (ego), they perceived themselves as part of a whole, not as individuals. The metaphors of the mind are the worlds it perceives. In a sense to understand the ancient world we must be prepared to abandon a few things, both ego and modern language, words we were given at birth to describe the world that existed before there were words to describe it. The age of matriarch or goddess are words we use to describe that ancient world, but the ancient world did not use those words to describe itself.

The ancient world can be better understood by considering it in terms of a Bicameral Mind this term was coined by Julian Jaynes. In his 1976 book "The Origin of Consciousness in the Breakdown of the Bicameral Mind," wherein he made the case that a bicameral mentality was the normal and ubiquitous state of the human mind from the beginning of time, up until as recently as 6000 years ago.

Loosely based on a hypothesis in psychology that argues that the human mind once assumed a state in which cognitive functions were divided between one part of the brain which was "speaking", and a second part which listens and obeys (the philosophy of "two-chambered nests" We have all grown up in a vastly different reality, indoctrinated in a patriarchal consciousness, our intrinsic ideas born of the men who designed them. They are indelibly etched into our consciousness, to the point

where we do not question the origins of our thoughts. In view of the times, it's imperative that we reconsider the history we have been fed.

Surely, if we keep doing what we have always done, we will reap what we sow. If we are to escape the cycle of repetitive problem, it's reasonable to first understand when and how those problems first began.

The historical record of Adam and Eve points to a change in human consciousness that occurred about six thousand years ago. After, as the good book states, the first human couple "disobeyed God," the Bible reports a drastic shift in human consciousness, In the book of Genesis, it says "Adam and Eve's eyes were opened, and they discerned that they were both in a state of nakedness and for this they felt shame." Was this the birth of the consciousness of self? Are Adam and Eve simply a metaphor that was used to describe a change in the human condition? Indigenous tribes throughout the world, whose allegories predate the Bible, they also have their stories of creation. In many cases their stories match closer to what scientists are claiming, regarding our genetic history.

The earliest known stories of human origin depict the creation of the universe by a woman not a man. A feminine Goddess named Eu-rynome, called "the Creator of All Things." Commenting on this in his classic study of the Greek Myths, Robert Graves states: "In this archaic religious system there were as yet neither gods nor priests, but only a universal goddess and her priestesses." In all myth throughout the world, the original Creator is feminine. It is only with the coming of a masculine-dominated (patriarchal) social system that a male god replaces her. Sometimes the goddess was slowly and methodically edged out, and the male God edged in. James Mellaart, quite possibly the world's foremost authority on Near Eastern archaeology, states that historically "the culture of the Great Goddess is "the basis of our civilization." Sites exemplifying this have been found in Spain, France, Germany, Austria, Czechoslovakia, Russia, and recently as far afield as Anatolia in the Near East. Some of these sites date back well over 25,000 years, and in these virtually all statues, the divine or human, are female.

However, with the invasion of Indo-European warrior nomads, Goddess-worshipping cultures were defeated, and their new rulers began subordinating Goddesses to Gods within the hierarchy of deities. While Goddess worship did not disappear completely at first, it tended to take a backseat to the worship of male war-Gods. During that time, pre-Christian Greek and Roman civilizations were already patriarchal, or male-dominated, and their religious pantheons were led by a father god whose wife remained subservient to him. Even the earlier Mycenaean society, which formed the early Greeks who conquered Troy, was patriarchal. In other words, the end of gender-egalitarian, Goddess-worshipping civilizations occurred more than 1500 years before Christianity.

In contrast to later cultures like Greece or Rome, the Minoans seem to have had little interest in war. There are no images of warfare or violence, and no weapons have been found in archeological remains. In fact, many archaeologists believe that ancient Crete was a peaceful and egalitarian society, which avoided the carnage of warfare for hundreds of years. This peace lasted until about 1,500 B.C. when warriors from mainland Greece invaded Crete, and Crete's culture began to decline. This is painfully obvious from the shift in artwork away from images of nature to images of warfare and anthropomorphic Gods.

Conceivably, one might think it is no coincidence that ancient Crete was a peaceful and nature-worshipping culture since women were in positions of power. Perhaps if more women were in higher status positions, there would be less conflict and competition, and more empathy and equality. However, it was likely not that simple. Women who hold high-status roles in our societies tend to take on typically "masculine" characteristics, such as competitiveness and emotional hardness. They become products of the patriarchal society having to sacrifice "femininity for survival." This is not their fault — if you want to succeed in a man's world, you must do so using the same tactics and characteristics as men. Looking back at cultures like ancient Crete can reveal what happens in a society when the balance of equality is shifted, and the egos, or self-centered and self-serving ideologies, are introduced. This cements a strong sense of individuality into the human psyche, which can make us feel disconnected from one another, from nature, and even from our bodies.

The main difference between the Minoans and other cultures such as the Greeks and the Romans lies in the former's lack of a strong ego. The Minoans felt strongly connected to nature and did not have the drive to accumulate power and wealth. This inner feeling of security and contentment came from having a strong connection to their environment. Their environment was their wealth, and from this secure state arose their great peace of mind.

In the 1960s, an archaeologist called Mallart led a team to excavate a site in Anatolia, Turkey. This site turned out to be the oldest city ever discovered. Known as *Catalo Hayek*, it goes back over 9,000 years. What the archaeologists discovered goes against everything they have previously learned about people living in Neolithic times. In fact, no weapons of war were found in the graves or anywhere else in the city. Furthermore, it was also a place full of feminine images, leading Mallart to believe that the people worshiped the Ancient Great Mother. Unfortunately, the site was shut down for thirty years, as these discoveries were too alarming.

The educational implications of findings such as these were widely ignored because the evidence did not validate the narrow, male-centric viewpoints asserting that only men can govern successfully. This attitude is detrimental to understanding the peace that humankind has lost. To learn from the past, we must first delve into the myths and religions developed by that society. Then, we can come to a greater understanding of what life must have been like, and thereby learn from others' mistakes by examining the changes wrought upon a society's myths throughout its history. If we consider the Neolithic Period of Egyptian religion and mythology, then trace the changes that occurred, as the years passed, we would see a pattern emerging — a slow, but steady power shift in the balance from women to men. The matriarchal period of ancient Egypt seems to have existed from prehistoric period up until Osiris' first appearance around c.3000 BC.

Matriarchy is a form of society in which power rests with the women and in particular with the mothers of a community. The word matriarchy is derived from the Latin word "*mater*" meaning "mother" and the Greek word "*archaic*" meaning "to rule." There also exists a different term for women's rule, namely "Gynecocracy," sometimes referred to as "Gynocracy."

The idea that women once ruled the world in ancient times is not a new thing. In the 19th century, Swiss jurist, writer and scholar named J.J Bachofen (1) assembled evidence of matriarchal societies in ancient times which made other scholars of the day strongly criticize him. However, the famous psychologist Carl Jung developed from it the theory that the ancient Great Mother was an important archetype. In 1861, Bachofen released *Das Mutterrecht*, the controversial book meaning "Mother-Right." Based on his study of mythology, he hypothesized that a peaceful, female-led, agrarian cultural society once prevailed throughout Europe and the Near East but the rise of militarism eventually resulted in a male takeover. Homer, the eighth-century B.C Greek poet, was the first to mention the existence of the Amazon rulers. In his poem, the *Iliad* — which was written during the Bronze/Heroic Age — Homer referred to the Amazonians as *antianginal*, an ambiguous term that has resulted in many different translations, from "antagonistic to men" to "the equal of men." In any case, Homer regarded these women as worthy opponents to his male characters as far as to boast of killing them without the men looking like cowardly bullies.[1]

After the first evidence of prehistoric societies where men did not dominate women was unearthed, many scholars of that time concluded that since they were not patriarchies, they must have been matriarchies. However, matriarchy is never the opposite of patriarchy, but the other side of a coin of the dominating model of a society. The real alternative to a patriarchal or male-dominant society is a structurally different way to organize social relations. This is the partnership model, where superiority or inferiority does not dictate the difference between male and female diversity.

Now, would the world be more peaceful if women were to be in charge? According to Harvard University psychologist, Steven Pinker, in his book — *The Better Angels of Our Nature* — he says the answer to that is "yes." Pinker presents data showing that human violence, which is still preeminent today, has been gradually declining. Furthermore, he states that, "Over the long sweep of history, women have been and will always be a pacifying force." He continued by "…Traditional war is a man's game — tribal women never assemble to raid neighboring villages." As mothers, women have evolutionary incentives to maintain peaceful conditions as to nurture their offspring and also to ensure the survival of their genes unto the next generation. The goddess "Hathor" personified the principles of joy, feminine love, and motherhood. She is strongly believed to be one of the most popular and most important deities throughout ancient Egypt.

There are no reports of wars or violence in history during ancient Egypt's matriarchal era, which as stated earlier extended from the pre-

[1] Foreman, Amanda: The Amazon Women: Is There Any Truth Behind the Myth? (2014).

historic era up until 3,000 B.C. But the gradual introduction of male deities into the society paralleled the slow penetration and then colonization of Egypt by foreigners from the north. However, the paradigm shift from a female-dominant society to a male-dominant one did not completely overtake Egypt until the beginning of the New Kingdom (around 1,570 BC) during the reign of Cleopatra. Cleopatra is believed to be the last woman to rule ancient Egypt.

Through shrewd politics, the founding fathers of the patriarchal network attempted to seize from her the kingdom she inherited from her father. Although young, Cleopatra was shrewd enough to appeal to Roman general, Julius Caesar, for help. After being expelled from her position as Pharaoh in Egypt, a young Cleopatra had herself delivered in an oriental rug to the palace of Julius Cesar in Alexandria. Julius Cesar fell in love with Cleopatra and agreed to help her take back her kingdom. Julius Caesar invaded Egypt with 20,000 soldiers, and he restored Cleopatra to the throne. However, through a series of conspiracies, assassinations, and betrayals, her kingdom was then retaken from her. Egypt, along with all of her resources (Africa at the time was a global gold supplier), eventually fell to the control of Rome.

During the Neolithic period, throughout all areas of the Nile and the Middle East, there appeared a widespread goddess system of worship. The basis of this is the recovery of the so-called numerous Venus figurines from widely scattered archaeological sites. The similarity of style in these figurines suggests that a resemblance of worship and rituals that could have existed. This goddess government could very well have been the origin of all ancient matriarchal societies, especially those that depended most on agriculture, such as Egypt and its neighbors up unto the northeast in Mesopotamia.

Riane Eisler is one of the most prominent writers on women's oppression and human liberation of our time. Her best-known book, *The Chalice and the Blade and The Power of Partnership*, describes the basic patterns regarding four dimensions: social structure, gender relations, the

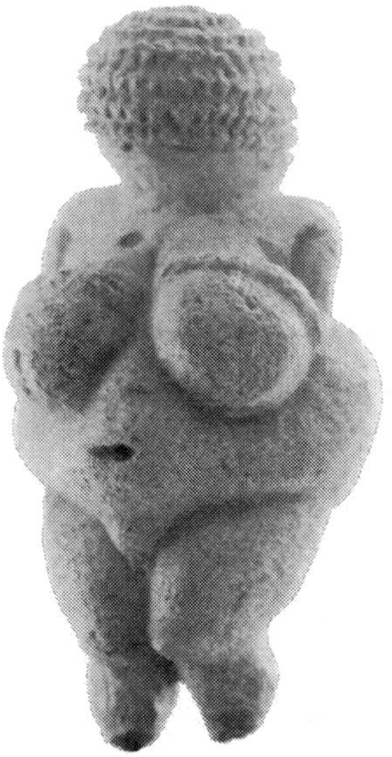

The artifact known as the Venus of Willendorf dates to between 24,000-22,000 B.C. making it one of the oldest and most famous surviving works of art representing the matriarch era.

emotional dimension, and value beliefs. In the domination model, hierarchies of domination (*i.e.*, rankings that sharply distinguish between those who are controlled and those who control), typically characterize social relations. In the partnership model, relationships tend to be egalitarian. Hierarchies exist, but they are what Eisler calls hierarchies of actualization. A synonym for actualization here is empowerment. The wiser, more experienced and skilled people assist the less experienced and less skilled people to acquire the capacities they lack.

In the domination model, the male half of humanity typically ranks above the female half. Traits and activities, such as control and conquest, are highly valued and associated with masculinity. We learn gender inequality at an early age. It becomes the model for other inequalities expressed, regarding religious and racial rankings. The partnership model regards maleness and femaleness equally. Traits such as empathy, non-violent interaction, and caregiving are valued in women and men and expressed in social policy. In this model, the emotion of fear is prominent. Violence is expected and, to some extent, encouraged towards people and groups considered inferior. In its extremes, we see it manifest in physical and emotional forms of spousal and child abuse, as well as the abuse of subordinates in a work environment by superiors.

Unlike the patriarchal domination model, the partnership model fosters trust. There is little emphasis on fear and little acceptance of violence against individuals or groups. Whereas the domination model presents relations of control/domination as good, the partnership model presents relations of partnership, mutual respect, and processes of negotiation as good. In the historical record, we can look at the clans of ancient Egypt as a model of gender partnership where the mother was the primary parent of her family. It is interesting to note that male-dominated cultures seem to exist only in so-called "civilized societies." Aboriginal tribes throughout the world still maintain a high regard for women and even worship feminine gods.

The era of male dominance, which has lasted for at least 7000 years, is now ending, and gender bias is slowly dissolving.

Chapter Two:
MEN ARE REALLY WOMEN WITH PENISES

English, like many languages has evolved considerably from its original definitions and terminologies. The term "man" was originally without gender. In ancient times it meant more or less the same things as the modernday word "person" The original English word "man" spoken by our ancestors, carried no distinction of male or female. About a thousand years ago this all began to gradually change. Mid-way through the 20th century, man became a male oriented terminology. Many English words were inspirited by the Germanic mother language; the word originally pronounced "were" was commonly used in reference to "male human." As in "werewolf," which meant, "man wolf."

The name we today apply exclusively to a married woman, "wife," (wif) at one time meant "female human without marital distinction." We can see from the wide range of variation of the original definitions of general human titles that language evolved as holistic human identity evolved.

The Hebrew term "adham" was a collective noun meaning humankind or humanity without reference to sex, race or other distinctions. In other words, it was not the male name, Adam as it is commonly understood today; rather it was a noun denoting more than one person. In fact Genesis 1:27–28 speaks of the creation of adham, making it clear that it is referring both to male and female, but distinct from being God.

Interestingly, however, women are the only one of the genders endowed with the powers of Godlike creation. Women alone have the propensity to reproduce asexually. In fact, it is not possible for men to produce an offspring without a female, meaning the ability to recreate itself through non-sexual reproduction This is the meaning of the term, Immaculate Conception, conceiving a child without a father or a biological equivalent, that is, to impregnate without sexual intercourse, asexual reproduction, or mitotic cell division (mitosis).

A perfect example of asexual reproduction was reported in the Journal of Fish Biology in 2008. It said: Scientists have confirmed the second case of a "virgin birth" in a shark. DNA testing had undeniably proved that a pup carried by a female Atlantic Blacktip shark in the Virginia Aquarium & Marine Science Center contained no genetic material from a male. However, even more astonishing is a recent discovery close to the coast of Florida, where seven Sawfish were experiencing virgin births. In fact, this is the first solid evidence of such asexual reproduction in the wild for any animal with a backbone, scientists added (Live Science, 2015).

Asexual reproduction rarely happens in vertebrates, but more and more instances are increasingly being discovered in the wild. For example, the Komodo dragon, the world's largest living lizard, has given birth via parthenogenesis (without a male). Such virgin births have also been seen, in birds such as chickens and turkeys, and in snakes such as pit vipers and boa constrictors (Live Science, 2015).

Hence, it is theoretically possible for women to reproduce or procreate without any male genetic contribution (i.e. sperm) while it is impossible for men to reproduce without women. Earlier it was mentioned that the female Komodo dragons, chickens, turkeys, and snakes could produce offspring by parthenogenesis. With that in mind, one might imagine that True Hermaphroditism, the presence of both male and female gonads in a single creature, may have once been the way we were.

The human fetal blueprint is initially undifferentiated, with the potential to become female, male, some variety thereof, or something entirely different. We all begin as a ball of cells that quickly differentiate into various body parts. The fetus at five weeks of gestation, sports a neural tube which will eventually become the neural spine, but other than that, it totally looks like a wad of bubble gum. Then at six weeks' gestation, the outlines of the face, eyes, arms and legs (and it's worthy to note that the tail also shows up for a while) appear. It won't be until about the sixth week that the fetus will start taking on the biological accouterments of sex.

If the fetus has a Y chromosome, the testosterone hormone will turn the buds of sexual organs into testes. Once in operation, those testes will consistently pump out even more testosterone and, voila, the penis begins to grow. On the other hand, female fetuses, not swayed by testosterone, will stay firm to the blueprint which calls for ovaries and a vagina. Fertility specialists have revealed a way for women to have babies without men. The process involves making a cocktail of chemicals acting as "artificial sperm" and then tricking a human egg (and the sperm) into forming an embryo like in normal human reproduction. The sperm, carrying 23 sets of chromosomes, fertilizes an egg carrying 23 pairs which leads to the building blocks of life. This crucial binding, creation of 46 pairs of chromosomes, opens the way for cell division, and this is the starting point of human life. However, researchers Dr. Yan-Ling Feng and Dr. Jerry Hall found a way through which eggs could duplicate their chromosomes as to create the number needed to begin cell division.

We were all initially asexual creatures; there was no sexual identity present at all during conception or in the early development stage of the fetus. By default, every human, in its pre-sexual assigned state, resembles a female. The x-y chromosome responded to the presence of testosterone or estrogen. After we were born, depending upon which culture we were domesticated into has a direct effect bearing upon our degree of masculinity. In actuality, both sexes are defined by apparel and grooming versus biology. We are now to a point where we imagine ourselves as a particular gender rather than an expression of the two.

Prenatal Differentiation of Internal Structures

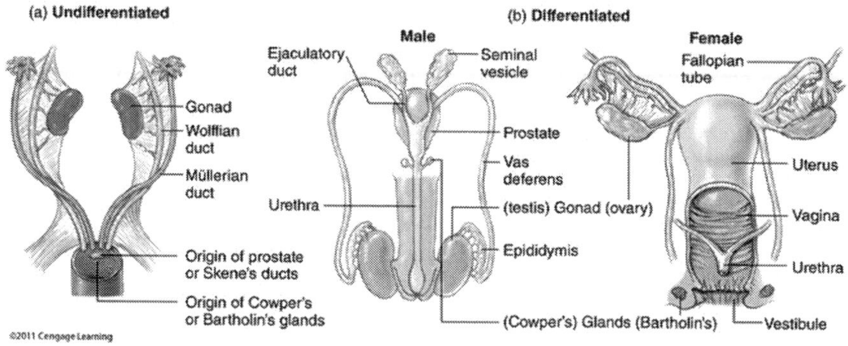

.Figure 2. Prenatal differentiation of internal reproductive structures

The idea of men being women with penises is just too absurd for even the wildest imagination to fathom. However, it is an undeniable fact, whether one can handle the truth or not, that men are the biological adaption of the female sex through the addition of a penis. Penises and clitorises are the same initial parts, which take on a different future based the presence of testosterone or estrogen. The female clitoris and male penis grow from the same genital tubercle and both enlarge when aroused. Before prenatal differentiation, the tubercle is neither a penis nor a clitoris — one of the only things determining whether it turns into one or the other is exposure to testosterone. Medically, the clitoris is said to be the homolog of the penis or the female counterpart of the penis. Some have oversimplified this by saying "the clitoris is just an under-developed penis." Well, now that we know that men prenatally had equal potential to turn into women, it might be just as accurate to say the penis is just an oversized clitoris. It is understandable why powerful men who control the scientific evidence try to cover up the facts for fear that the feminine energies will once again dominate the planet. However, the DNA evidence is clear; it shows that Adam and Eve could not have existed in the ways the Bible portrays them.

Genetic data shows no evidence of humanity arising from two people; there are simply too many different varieties of genes around for that to make sense. A further look into human genes reveals a different genetic history for Adam and Eve. Mitochondrial DNA points to the genes in this organelle tracing back to a single female ancestor who lived about 140,000 years ago. However, those genes on the Y chromosome (Adam) trace back to one male who lived as recently as 60,000–90,000 years ago.

This shows not only that "Adam" and "Eve" (in the sense of mito-chondrial and Y-chromosome DNA alone) must have lived thousands of years apart, but also that there simply could not have been two individuals who provided the entire genetic ancestry of modern humans.

The implications for these genetic studies are, in short, revolutionary, indicating that there were no men "In the beginning!" In fact, it is not likely that Y-chromosome Adam and Mitochondrial Eve lived within the same generation; and no studies to date indicate that they arrived at the same time.

When we analyze the Biblical story of Eve (the Genesis account of creation) and the Gospel account of the virgin birth) we can fit together a fairly accurate chronology of the path of human origins from a genetic, scientific perspective. Mitochondria Eve, the mother of all civilization, possesses the rare ability to self-replicate herself. This process is called parthenogenesis (virgin birth). Genetic science points to two different time periods for the origination of the (x) female chromosomes and the (y) male, indicating that they lived 65,000 years apart from each other, with the X being the older of the two genomes. Unlike any woman living today Mitochondria Eve produced offspring without a male sperm donor. Meaning the earlier class of woman of African origin had genetic potential for asexual reproduction, she was unique in that the genetic potential to self-reproduce was not passed on to her distant offspring. She is part of a relatively extinct class of woman that made up what's called in genetic anthropology"the founder effect". The founder effect exists where there are greater genome variations between the found-

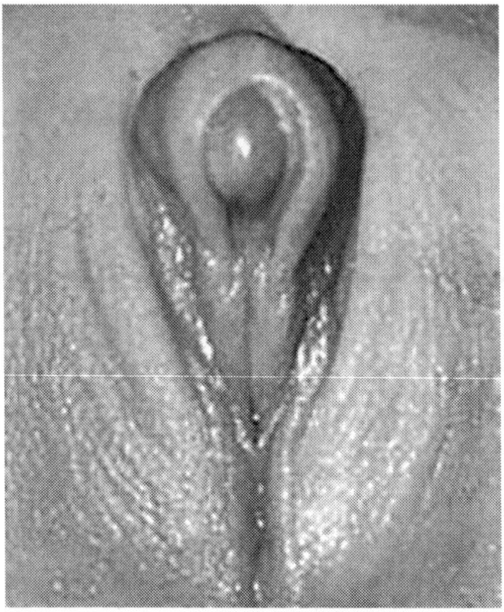

Figure 6. Ambiguous genitalia with what appears to be both a penis and a vaginal opening and Labia Majora

ing fathers of a colony, than the offspring of the founders (their distant children). A good example can be gleaned from the concept of race. Although people of European and African decent may appear very different in appearance from each other because of skin tone and the shapes of their features (eyes, ears, nose) they are actually genetically closer relatives than earlier humans that make up the founders who held higher variations within the gene pool, thus allowing for what we today call inbreeding without genetic complications. The original feminine being the roots of human civilizations can be thought of as a class of virgins, used to prime the human gene pool into sexual reproduction.

In the Dominican Republic and Papua New Guinea, relatively large populations of female children become males within a few months of reaching puberty. During the 1970s, 1 in 90 males in the Dominican Republic had a condition known as 5-Alpha-Reductase Deficiency. Unbeknownst to the parents their daughters were, in fact, males. They appeared to be female with a vagina and the tenderness of a little girl and were raised as young girls. However, when they hit puberty; their testicles descended, the phallus grew, their voice deepened, muscle and bone mass increased, and they transform into men.

According to discoveries, children with these rare genetic characteristics typically have underdeveloped testes and penis hidden in the body cavity. The Y chromosome and various important hormones and enzymes are what program the development of the male genitalia and ensure that a male fetus develops into a male child. Even with these incredible scientific, and particularly medical, findings, it seems that the general human population still does not accept the possibility of various human expressions, while we look down upon, stigmatize, and categorize what exists.

In time, humanity has to some extent reconsidered or moderated its views on homosexuality and transgendered individuals. If in the ever changing world of human genomes, a child that looks and acts like a girl can turn into a fertile and functioning young man, doesn't that leave the door open for the possibility that gender variations such as Klinefelter's Syndrome (XXY), Turner Syndrome (XO), Fetally Androgenized Females (XX female fetus that was exposed to androgens in utero) and, transgenderism, may not be choices after all, but also natural parts of human expression? In fact, the term "natural" really means; "existing in or caused by nature; not made or caused by humankind." Essentially this obviously means that all of the above mentioned "conditions" are in fact natural; not accidents of nature; they are just variations.

In fact, there are many reasons for variations of what we expect as the "natural" creation of biological sex. For example, mitochondria are located in the tail of the sperm; they provide it with that whip like energy to move. Mitochondria carry out aerobic respiration that produces energy in the form of ATP molecules (adenosine triphosphate). These are important in helping the sperm remain mobile so it can have sufficient energy to reach the oviduct/ fallopian tube where it will fertilize the egg.

In most multicellular organisms, mitochondria are inherited from the mother. Both eggs and sperm have mitochondria in them, but as mentioned before, the mitochondria in the sperm are located in the tail and do not enter the egg during reproduction — therefore children only receive mitochondrial DNA from their mothers. Mitochondrial DNA passes to all offspring, but only daughters can pass it on. Scientists have been able to determine that a single woman, who lived around 150,000 years ago, is associated with all humans alive today. They have also been able to trace how people moved out of Africa and into the rest of the world using mtDNA. In fertilization, a sperm pretty much only contributes its DNA. Everything else that makes up a cell (called the cytoplasm) comes from the egg. Since mitochondria are in the cytoplasm, it makes sense that they come from the egg. In her research, Gender Metamorphosis at Work (2005) Elizabeth Kelly wrote:

In the 1970s, Julianne Imperato, Ph.D., of Cornell University traveled to the Dominican Republic to investigate claims of young female-appearing children developing masculine features. The locals referred to the phenomena by two names: Guevedoces, translated to mean "penis at age twelve," and Machihembras, meaning "first a woman, then a man." In the following years, reports suggested that this was also common in the Zambian villages of Papua New Guinea, where the locals called these individuals Turnips, meaning, "expected to become men."

The Guevedoces, Machihembras, and Turnips are born with an XY genotype and both sex chromosomes intact. During fetal development, the sex-determining region of the Y chromosome (SRY) inhibits female internal sexual organ development and induces the development of internal male sexual organs. In the past, people regarded guevedoche as females and raised them as such. As any normal male would, gueved-oche has a sudden increase in testosterone levels during puberty, which may cause the clitoris to enlarge. This surge of testosterone, in turn, may be responsible for the initiation of normal male sexual development and often results in the growth of facial and body hair and the deepening of the voice. Subsequently, most guevedoche spends their adult years resembling sexually normal males, though subtle differences still exist. For example, most guevedoche have decreased amounts of facial hair and smaller prostate glands about the average male.[2]

Research has shown this genetic variation to be of autosomal recessive inheritance. Due to the decreased size of the gene pool in these com-

[2] E, Kelley; the Guevedoces

munities as well as their isolation from other populations, this gender expression persists for generations.

During the 1970s, Guevedoces births were reported to account for as many as two percents of all births in these small villages of the Dominican Republic. Since then, doctors in villages in both the Dominican Republic and Papua New Guinea have become experts in distinguishing normal female external genitalia from the ambiguous genitalia of Guevedoces babies. Due to the prevalence of these births, both cultures believe in three sexual categories: the male, the female, and the pseudohermaphrodite.

The differences in the way these two societies deal with this rare occurrence reveal the magnitude to which a society's culture can affect an individual's beliefs and opinions. The Zambians view these children as flawed males; families and the society reject and humiliate the chil-

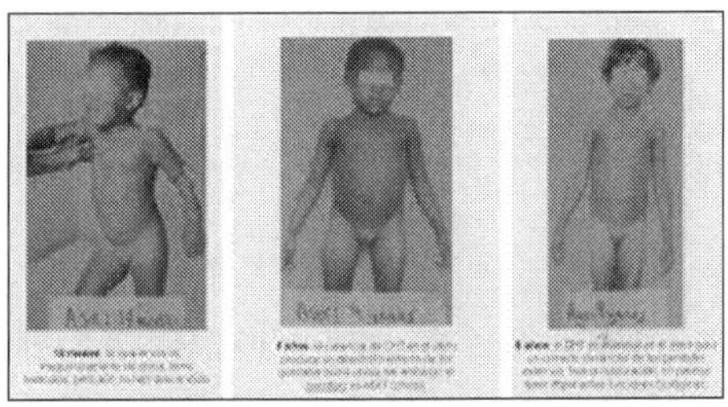

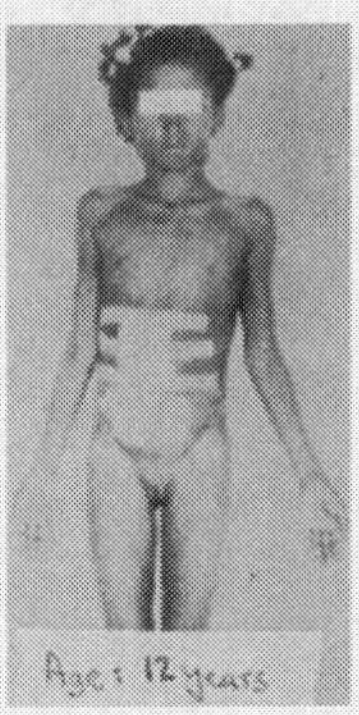

12 años: justo antes de la pubertad, antes de que la testosterona irrumpa, el fenotipo todavía es el de una chica.

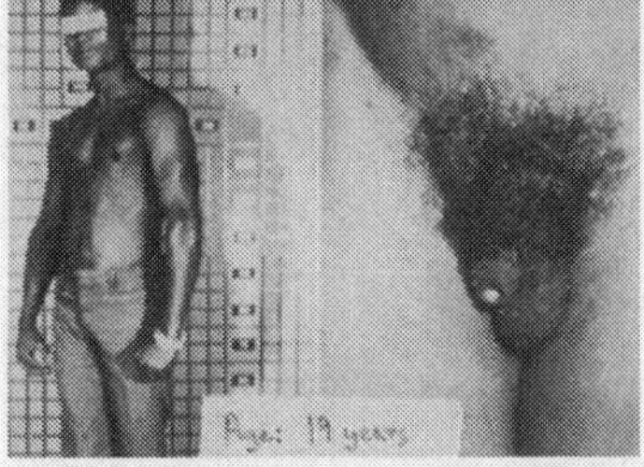

19 años: con el surgimiento de la testosterona en la pubertad, el fenotipo cambia a hombre, la voz se hace grave, los testículos descienden, el pene crece y comienzan la erección y eyaculación. Se desarrolla la orientación masculina psicosexualmente.

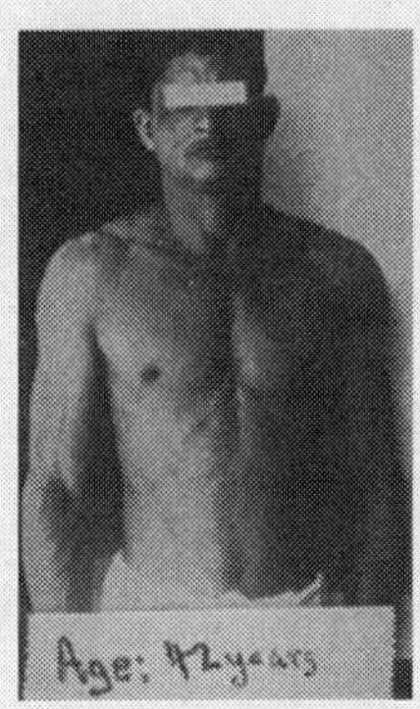

42 años: son hombres el resto de su vida, aunque con escasa barba, carencia calvicie, ausencia de acné y próstata pequeña.

dren. On the other hand, in the Dominican Republic, the birth of a pseudohermaphrodite is fully accepted, and during puberty, a joyous celebration marks the child's physical transformation into a male. The Dominican Republic communities that quietly accept their Guevedoces citizens are a model for the world on how to deal with genetic differences; they are showing us how to support and help a person have a full and rewarding life despite being different.

Chapter Three: IS PENIS ENVY REALLY VAGINA ENVY?

Sigmund Freud's views on women's cognitive development stirred much controversy during his lifetime and continued to evoke considerable debate and concern to this day. Freud viewed women simply as a man without a penis. Stemming from this theory, Freud coined the phrase "Penis Envy" and claimed Penis Envy is a problem woman could never resolve because they cannot change the fact that they do not have a penis. Freud's theory contends that during the phallic stage, roughly between ages 3-5, young girls distance themselves from their mothers and devote their affections to their fathers. According to Freud, this occurs when a girl realizes that she has no penis. He further contends that little girls hold their mother responsible for their lack of a penis. Eventually, though, these little girls grow up to live in the silent shadows of male authority and privileged.

His radical ideas were more than a harmless, innocent theory; they became the foundation of the emerging science of public manipulation called "propaganda. Freud and his nephew Edward Bernays, used the theory of penis envy, to manipulate mass consciousness, and further their economic ambitions. In brief, Edward Bernays was an advertising guru. In what was called a clever rogue, he promoted his uncle, Sigmund Freud as the father of Psychology then he promoted his uncle's theories

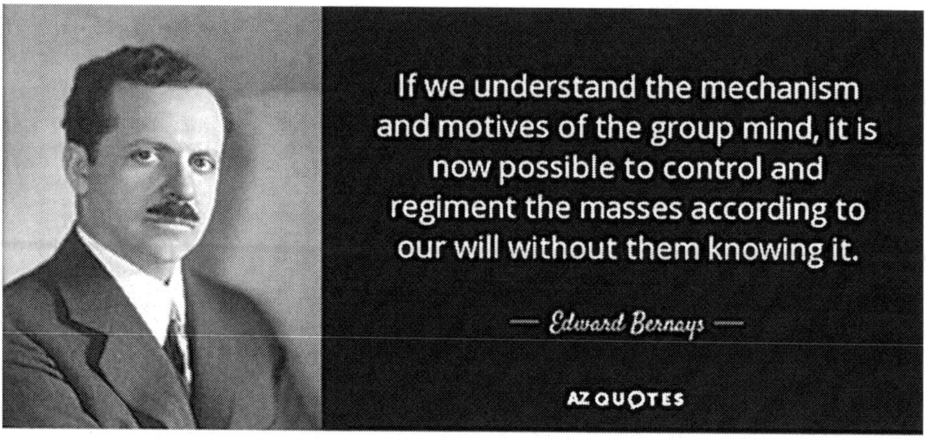

in commercial advertising. The tobacco industry became one of their clients, interested in increasing sales and increasing profits; they hired Edward Bernays to use Freud's theories to get women to start smoking.

The "Torches of Freedom" campaign was the brainchild of Edward Bernays, using the psychology of his uncle, Sigmund Freud, and fueled with money from the tobacco industries. He organized a campaign designed to encourage women to smoke cigarettes by exploiting women's aspirations for a better life during the women's liberation movement in the United States. Bernays described cigarettes as symbols of emancipation and equality with men. Cigarettes became an avenue for women to challenge social norms and fight for equal rights as men. The cigarette came to symbolize "rebellious independence, glamor, seduction and sexual allure for both." During this era, the women's equality movement was in its infancy. Women were challenging male dominance.

We have come a long way from Freud's narrow centric viewpoint. The patriarchs of Freud's era held the view of female inferiority, based on the sin of Eve. Women have struggled for thousands of years to overcome the early disposition of being branded as the Jezebel, the cursed seed of Eve. Sigmund Freud was not a compassionate person in this area, by his admission he was oblivious to woman's needs. Freud called this "The great question that has never been answered," Despite his thirty years of research into the feminine soul he admits that he didn't understand "'what does a woman want?' The biggest problem with the patriarch reality is that it is confined to self-interest and blinded to the interest of others. What was elaborately theorized as penis envy in Freud's world view was the natural desire for freedom and equality that all humans yearn for. The male privilege was attached to the notion that men were in charge of the world and free to do as they wished while women were subjugated as property.

A man's greatest weakness is a woman. Given what we universally understand today about the general weakness of men in the area of sexuality, it's reasonable to challenge Freud's theory and ask the question. Are men in a general sense the one suffering from womb envy? Is there emptiness in his soul? — An inward mourning of the evolutionary loss of his vagina? Could this explain the desire to control the vagina of their wives and girlfriends? Could his need to control the vagina stem from the loss of his own? As long as there has been recorded history, many men have demonstrated an uncontrollable urge to control the vagina, by any means necessary, going as far as making the subjugation of the feminine a social norm.

Patriarchy propaganda pamphlet. USA, circa 1933

The fact that Prostitution is purported to be the oldest profession in the world is a strong indicator of just how long society has been unbalanced. Prostitution is fueled by the world that does not afford women economic equality, as well as a man's willingness to rent part of a woman's body. By maintaining a male-dominated society where men always control the purse, men are also able to control women. Knowing that women deprived of their basic needs will seek desperate measures for survival is a large reason why inequality is woven into the everyday existence of most societies. It is not an accident; it is by design. Up until the legalization of birth control pills in 1967, it was commonplace for women to spend the first 18 years of their lives under their father's roof. Their destiny was then typically to marry, having no other choice but to bear children and spend the rest of their lives under their husband's servitude.

"A man's home is his castle", and under the spell of imperialism many men came and still come from homes that reinforce this dysfunctional viewpoint.

In 1943, Abraham Maslow wrote a theory highly respected in the field of psychology called "The Hierarchy of Needs" which simply stated that if a persons' basic physiological requirements for security, food, shelter and clothing are not met the individual will become psychologi-

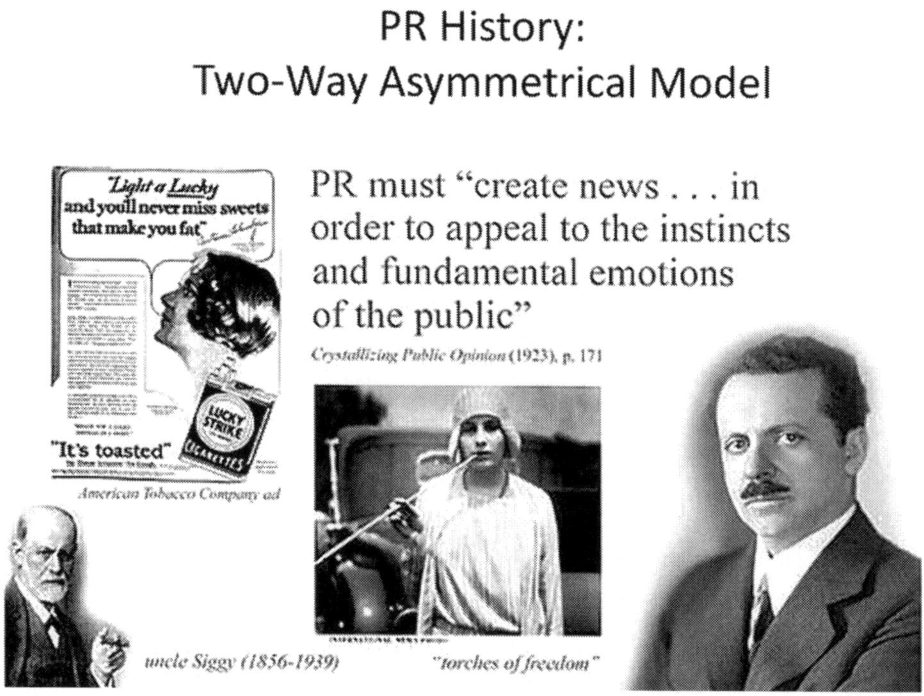

cally crippled from thriving equally in society. Such has been the case of the women- cast into the bottom rung of Maslow's Hierarchy of Needs. The prostitution culture is driven by the men that created it. This is a secret aspect of most societies around the world. They have their hidden locations where men can go to relieve sexual tension.

A man in a small village in India was interviewed outside of a popular brothel about his preoccupation with sex. He said, "Thank God that some women submit to prostitution because if they were not there to satisfy the desires of men, then more men would be raping woman." This quote goes to show the preoccupation with vagina many men have.

Why do some men crave vagina energy so much to the point of paying for sex or raping a woman? Why are some men willing to sacrifice reputation, honor, and self-respect, for the desire to place their penis inside of a woman's body? Marvin Gaye called it sexual healing, and one way or another in the case of many men, he's got to have it, as if some uncontrollable force had closed his mind and taken over his body.

Contrary to what Freud postulated in his theory of penis envy, it seems more likely that many men may suffer from vagina envy. The terms womb envy and vagina envy denote the anxiety that many men may feel caused by envy of the biological functions of the female sex: pregnancy, parturition, breastfeeding and the general power that women have to bring life into the world. For centuries the desire among men for the vaginal body part, along with breast and buttocks, has been so intense that men have gone as far as to take sex by force.

Rape stems from control. As man seeks to control something that he does not have (a vagina), men have been deemed so weak by society in the area of sex, that women have been blamed for man's weakness as if his weakness was also his alibi. Is the real weakness envy, jealousy of a women's reproductive system? Many times, we find when men are insistent upon domination they do so really because they feel weak. Yet, because of the present potential of danger, a woman must be careful of which types of garment she wears, or she might find herself blamed for seduction- the mere presence of femininity could arouse fiery desires that render him temporarily insane. What is it about the woman? Particularly the vagina, that hold so much power over men?

The shape of the vaginal is easily one of the most significant designs of ancient and modern times. The geometric shape of the vagina, called "the Vesica Pisces," was respected by our ancestors as the point where life comes into existence, a cosmic portal. The feminine is the matrix of this process, out of the particle and waves of her very existence flesh and blood and spirit emerge, she alone can conceive and give birth, participating in the greatest mystery of the cosmos, bringing a soul into life.

The womb shape of the female sexual organ is the blueprint of life itself. It is the almond shaped geometric design of the eyes, nostrils, ears and mouth, both hemisphere of the brain. Look carefully at your skin it is made up of trillions of vagina-shaped cones. 3-dimensional shapes with flat faces. The faces are congruent, regular polygons representing the creative signature of the feminine. Long before Christians used the sign of the fish to symbolize Jesus Christ, the Vesica Pisces was the symbol for bringing life into existence The Vesica Pisces was the all encompassing womb of life which embraced the 'unborn' and prepared them for an illumined birth. A Pythagorean symbol of the intersection of the world of the divine with the world of matter. The Vesica Pisces served as an appropriate symbol for the vagina representing the feminine creative force, the Mother-Spirit birthing gods, and worlds. It also carried the meaning of the "seat of the female sexual power."

It is often seen in medieval Christian art as a clear frame around holy figures and was called Mandorla (literally meaning "Almond"). Images of the Christ are often depicted bordered by the Vesica Pisces shape, as if in the posture of being birthed.

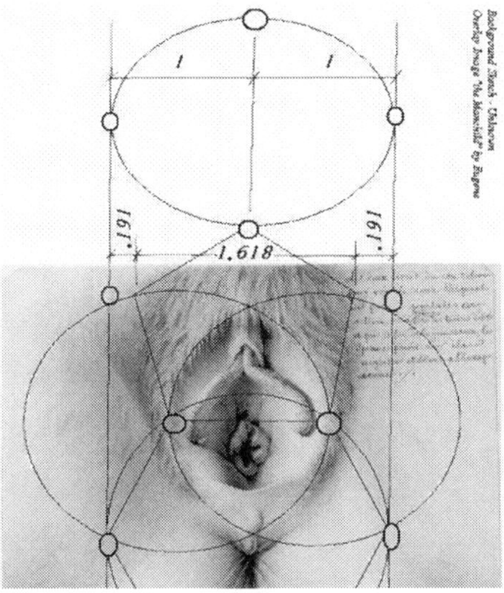

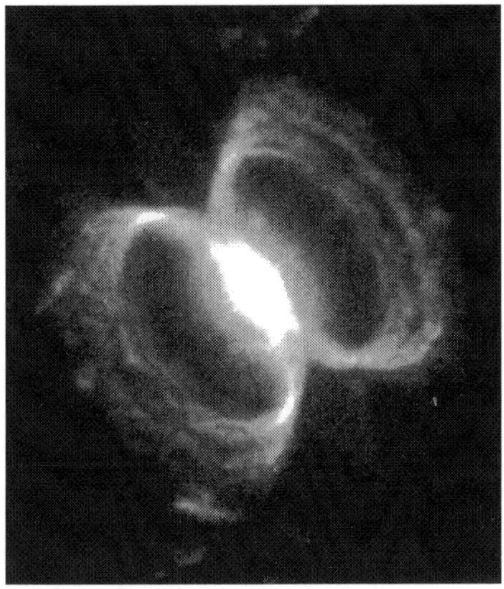

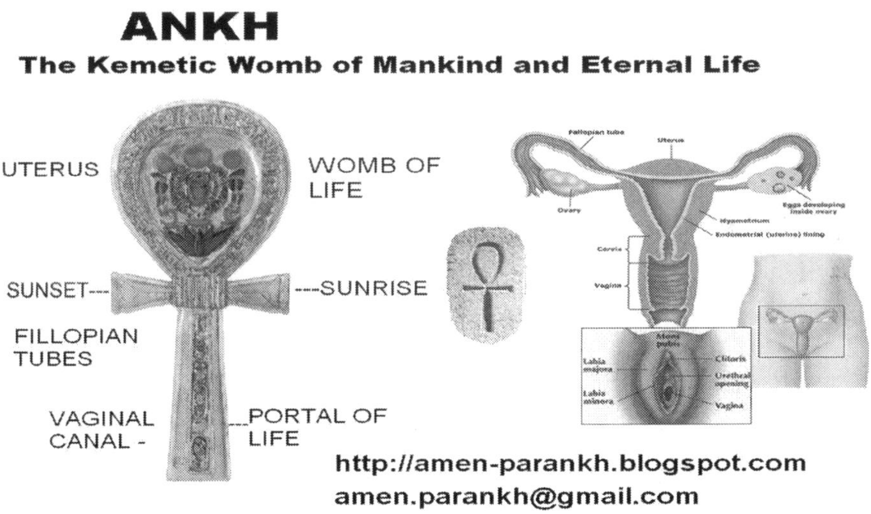

The Birds the Bees and the Vesica Pisces

Some people have called the Vesica Pisces the eye of God because it is the place where all things begin and come into existence. The Vesica Pisces is a literal cosmic portal, a stargate of transformation. Our five senses: sight (eyes), sound (ears), smell (nose), taste (mouth) and feeling (skin) are all translated through openings fashioned from the most ancient blueprint of life itself, the Vesica Pisces. Through these magical openings, vibrations and light are turned into the sounds and pictures our brains process to bring the world into our reality.

At the inner core of our ears, decibels of sound waves are translated into language. The energies from our sense of smell illicit feelings and pheromones which can be translated into actions and desires too numerous to mention, all through portals called the Vesica Pisces. From these much overlooked portals of transformation and information, an unending cycle of life can manifest. The point here is the Vesica Pisces, which is also called the womb of life, is the genesis point of all existence. Let's take a closer look at the role of the Vesica Pisces in our physical manifestation into this reality. The physical womb, also known as the Vagina, is the portal through which all humans have arrived into this experience.

The female womb is the most sought after property the world has ever known. Throughout history, men have fought wars, conquered empires and even built chastity belts to protect the temple and covet the Holy Grail of their most ardent desires. Drugs and alcohol have been used so that men could trap, drug and lay siege to her temple. Men and even some women spend many days of their lives, strategizing, fantasizing and dreaming about being in the womb, plotting they return to that Shangri-La location of the soul; the tranquil place of peace and solitude that was our first home.

Through a probe called the penis, men are magnetically drawn to experience the great ecstasy that emerges from inserting the penis into any number of Vesica Pisces shaped openings in a woman's body. It could be said that while women may have unconditional love for the sake of her love for humanity (that emerges through her cosmic portal), men tend to love and experience love mainly through her cosmic portal. As objectifying as this may seem, it is a common reality. Men equate sex with love and are usually surprised later when they find out their desires have translated into the miracle of bringing new life into the world. We are responsible for the world we see and the world we cannot yet see.

In the microscopic, invisible realm a single tiny sperm penetrates a woman's unfertilized egg causing an implosion of light or energy in its center (that is visible under the microscope, via infrared photography). One could say this is the moment when the spirit enters matter. The size of the egg itself in comparison to the humble sperm speaks volumes.

There are different schools of thought regarding the moment of conception or epigenesis. Does a single sperm carry an electrical charge to the egg, or is it purely chemical? Can the electrical charge, or chemical formula for that matter, be artificially reproduced? Considering how little it takes to stimulate an unfertilized egg into activity, it doesn't seem out of the realm of possibilities that a woman, in a state of sacred dance/trance ceremony, couldn't self-conceive. Before we agree or disagree with that thought, let's take a closer look at traditional conception.

During sexual intercourse, semen is released into the womb of life which fertilizes eggs released during the period of ovulation. Unlike sperm, which is produced daily throughout a lifetime, a woman's eggs are finite. To be more precise, during fetal life, there are about 6 million to 7 million eggs. At birth, this number is reduced to 1 million eggs, and by the time of puberty, only about 300,000 remain. Of these 300,000 eggs, only 300 to 400 will be ovulated during a woman's reproductive lifetime. Fertility drops as a woman ages due to decreasing number and quality of the remaining eggs. Within 12 hours of the egg and the sperm meeting, the egg begins the first cell division in the making of a human being called "mitosis division during mitosis, a cell duplicates all its contents, including its chromosomes, and splits to form two identical daughter cells.

Scientists have photographed these breathtaking phenomena of the first cell's divide and again we can plainly see the Vesica Pisces shape located in the center of the split. The identical image can be seen in virtually every medieval church in Europe. The churches were to be a place for the transformation of sinners to the saint. The fact many of these churches were dedicated to the Virgin Mary or Mary Magdalene (aka the Goddess), is part of this understanding. It is evident from the reoccurring symbol of femininity that women are an intricate part of creation that has a sacred role in the process of life.

Chapter Four:
THE FUTURE BEGINS IN HER WOMB

Only when we are brave enough to explore the darkness can we gain the infinite understanding that stems from light. A light dearly needed to reverse the damage caused by thousands of years of Patriarchal domination. During an era of profound darkness, the early fathers of Church and State sought through trial and error to understand the art of healing, this began the long and arduous plight of ancient medicine. Before this chromos, the position of the healer was held primarily by women, respectively called midwives, children of a gathering class of matriarchs that existed from the founding of Humanity, who taught the ways of natural healing through, herbs, roots, song, dance and other sacred ceremonial ritual.

However, beginning about 500 BC that way of life began to change. The institution we today call medicine was just getting started, and the term "Hysteria" was rapidly gaining popularity In Europe and later in the Americas hysteria was one of the first medical conditions ever diagnosed by doctors with no formal medical training. A wide range of symptoms met the criteria of "hysteria" such as fainting, sexual frustration, sexual desire, anxiety, depression, sleeplessness, irritability, nervousness and "a tendency to cause trouble for others was readily misdiagnosed as hysteria. This practice went on for hundreds of years. Looking back, it is reasonable to admit that the hysteria diagnosis was used as a thinly veiled method of policing women's sexuality, dismissing female voices, reducing women's potential credibility in public or professional spheres, and keeping women under control.

With the birth of patriarchal authority came the doctrine which taught that women were in a fallen condition due to sin. This view of female inferiority developed slowly after the fall of the Matriarchal rule, and coinciding with the rise of patriarchy, men who were instrumental in silencing the feminine voice in society ignited the rumor that women were physically and theologically inferior beings.

Aristotle (320 BC) was one of the early philosophers that cemented this flowering doctrine of male superiority into the mainstream: Aristotle's assertions that "woman was a failed man." He further asserts that the male is by nature superior and the female inferior, the male ruler and the female subject. The inferiority of women is considered by him and many patriarch leaders of that time a consequence of the sin of Eve. Hence, hysteria, also known as Uterine melancholy, emerged as a general diagnosis of a condition that arose as a direct result of the sin of Eve, thus from a patriarchal standpoint every woman was vulnerable to hysteria because every woman was the offspring of Eve.

The 2nd-century Roman physician Galen believed sexual deprivation caused hysteria. The term hysteria comes from the Greek word hysteria, which means the womb or uterus. The ancient medical establishment thought that the uterus was a free, peregrinating organ and that it was wandering about the woman's body causing hysteria; the good doctor recommended a good roll in the hay as a suitable cure for married women, but for widows, unmarried women, or religious women, he prescribed pelvic massage. Physicians would cite this technique for centuries to come.

Plato's, argument on the root causes of hysteria was that the uterus is sad because it's not joined with the male penis and does not give rise to a new birth. Another cause was thought to be the retention of a supposed female semen, thought to mingle with male semen during intercourse. This was believed to be stored in the womb. Hysteria was referred to as "the widow's disease" since the female semen was believed to turn venomous if not released through regular climax or intercourse

Hippocrates (5th century BC) considered by many to be the father of modern medicine also believed that the cause of this disease lies in the movement of the uterus.

The Greek physician provides an indepth hypothesis of hysteria, which he distinguished from epilepsy. He emphasizes the difference between the compulsive movements of epilepsy, caused by a disorder of the brain, and those of hysteria due to the abnormal movements of the uterus in the body. Then, he resumes the idea of a restless and migratory uterus and identifies the cause of the indisposition as stagnant poisonous humor which, due to an inadequate sexual life, have never been expelled.

He asserts that a woman's body is physiologically cold and wet and hence prone to putrefaction of the humor (as opposed to the dry and warm male body). For this reason, the uterus is likely to get sick, especially if it is deprived of the benefits arising from sex and procreation, which, widening a woman's canals, promote the cleansing of the body. And he goes further; especially in virgins, widows, single, or sterile women, this "bad" uterus — since it is not satisfied — not only produces toxic fumes but also takes to wandering around the body, causing various kinds of disorders such as anxiety, sense of suffocation, tremors, sometimes even convulsions and paralysis. For this reason, he suggests that even widows and unmarried women should get married and live a satisfactory sexual life within the bounds of marriage.

The studies dedicated to understanding hysteria took medicine into the area of psychology and is the basis of what we today call "psychiatry;" the early students of mental health began to be called psychiatrists after establishing a link between, sexual frustration, hysteria, and mental disorders. The procedure known as a hysterectomy (removal of the uterus) was believed to be a cure for acute patients suffering from hysteria. A woman could be deemed insane and committed to a mental institution against her will based upon charges by her spouse that hysteria was suspected. If the future world does not learn from past mistakes, it is destined to duplicate them.

If the women are permitted to control their own destiny, they will be the ones to decide the genetic makeup of the children of the future world they give birth to, allowing them to have control over the demographics of societies of the future. That is unless their options are suppressed by legislation. As of Feb 1, 2016, Britain's scientists were given permission for experiments with genetically modified human tissue. Around 7.9 million children each year are born with serious birth defects that have a significant genetic contribution. The logic is that if we could safely and easily correct these errors at the embryonic stage, it would be possible to eradicate this disease burden virtually. Many see meddling with our genome as inherently dangerous — no matter which genes we target.

It is believed that tampering with the gene pool will cause large ripples and those ripples uncontrollable consequences. According to this view, it would be far wiser not to open Pandora's Box. But some might reason, isn't the gene pool already violent? Embryo gene editing is a highly controversial topic. Some believe it provides an invaluable way to prevent genetic diseases at birth, while others think it will eventually lead to 'designer babies' and other unethical uses, as well as affecting the evolution of future generations in ways that can't possibly be predicted. Either way, we will be seeing genetically modified humans within our lifetime that is for sure. In fact, they are already here. Through the marvels of science, all the undesirable traits that exist within homegrown humans can be genetically modified out- just like with GMO foods. This includes a predisposition toward violence and socially unacceptable behavior, such as racism. This process is called "germline." It

has already been used with children predisposed to birth defects around the nation. About thirty of these "New Children" already exist and are about to graduate from High School.

The first successful transfer of genetic material for this purpose was published in a U.S. medical journal in 1997 and then later cited in a Human Reproduction publication in 2001. Scientists injected 30 embryos with a third persons' genetic material. The children who have been produced by this method have extra snippets of mitochondrial DNA, or mtDNA, from two mothers — meaning these babies technically have three parents. It's still unclear whether all 30 babies turned out healthy. The promoters of a designer-baby future believe that the new human genetic and reproductive technologies are both inevitable and a boon to humanity. They exuberantly describe near term genetic manipulations-within a generation that may increase resistance to diseases, "optimize" height and weight and boost intelligence.

Further off, but within the lifetimes of today's children, scientists foresee the ability to adjust personality, design new body forms, extend life expectancy, and endow hyperintelligence. Some even predict splicing traits from other species into children. In late 1999 for example, an

ABC Nightline special on human cloning speculated that genetic engineers would learn to design children with "night vision from an owl" and "supersensitive hearing cloned from a dog." This raises at least two issues. The first is the ethical issue surrounding the use of human embryos for scientific research, and associated concerns around creating designer babies. The second is the fact that this editing went so wrong in so many embryos. Without total control of the DNA editing process, the outcome for a baby born from a technology like this one is completely unknown.

An additional issue is what is to become of the old home grown humans? Will homegrown, unmodified humans be the target of discrimination for the mere fact that they have the propensity to commit acts of behavior consistent with their genetic predisposition? Will this be the new racism? Many see genetically modified humans as the promotion of the same eugenics used to justify genocide in Nazi Germany and feel that the public would never allow this. However, a recent development appears to have slipped under the public's' radar: human prenatal diagnosis. Screening fetal genomes to eliminate genetic 'defects' may lead to incremental changes in the human genetic reservoir: a permanent shift in our characteristics and eventually, self-domestication. The rate of the home-grown humans solving their social differences (racism) is slower than sciences' ability to make progress in genetically modifying future generations. In the end, women are the ones that have the last say over this procedure. But only if they are first given the power to say no, meaning that this would depend on a woman having control over what happens with their body.

Before the advent of the scientific method and modern medicine, women of old were the doctors and midwives, and the methods they used in healing involved the drinking of menstrual blood. One of the most important rituals in the old religion carried on by a woman of the druid period was the preparation of a 'drink of immortality' made from menstrual blood, which is full of healing stem cells, It was believed that this sacred ritual was the secret to health and longevity. In most ancient myths and religions, throughout the world dating back hundreds of thousands of years, the power of rebirth had always been a blessing of the Feminine Womb it had never been held by a man. Taoists priest believed a man could become immortal, or at least long-lived, by absorbing menstrual blood, called red yin juice, from a woman's Mysterious Gateway, a symbol of life-giving female energy. Chinese sages called this red juice the essence of Mother Earth, the yin principle that gives life to all things. They claimed the Yellow Emperor became a God by absorbing the yin juice of twelve hundred women.

Although there are many legends about the 'menstrual powers of female shamans' being stolen by male god Menstrual Mysteries — this was eventually censored, declared a heresy and women were barred from participating in Christian rites. It's difficult to ignore the similarities between the rituals of drinking the blood of the Christ that was incorporated into Christianity and the drink of immortality prepared by witches. It's said that the cup that Jesus drank from at the last supper called the Holy Grail was actually in its true original essence, the Womb from which all life emerged. The envy that many men felt or feel for the powers produced from women's bodies underlies much of the motive behind silencing her powers. After the men defeated the Goddesses, they began imitating menstruation with their own bodies and pretending to give birth (for example, the story of Zeus giving birth to the Goddess Athena from his brow; the Middle Eastern god Marduk who slew the Goddess Tiamat and from the pieces of her body grew the world; or the Christian God "speaking" the universe into existence). As the male imitation of menstruation in a society is acted out more blatantly and as men come into more control of the powers women created and formerly controlled, authentic menstruation itself is driven underground.

Chapter Five:
A CASE FOR EVE

A"ll wickedness, when compared to the wickedness of woman, is nothing. What else is a woman but a foe, an inescapable punishment, a necessary evil, a natural temptation, a desirable calamity, domestic danger, and a delectable detriment, an evil nature, painted with fair colors? Women are by nature instruments of Satan - they are by nature carnal, a structural defect rooted in the original creation."

Catholic Inquisition Authorities in 1485-86

Whether you believe the Bible was divinely inspired or not, you have to agree that the curse of Eve has enforced a negative connotation against women worldwide, despite the baseless nature of the claim. (Where in the world will anyone be asked to entertain a story involving a talking snake as an alibi?) As the quote at the beginning of this chapter states, Eve represents the fundamental character flaw in all women. She is the mold from which all women were cut. The words and actions of one woman have been used stereotypically to interpret the premeditated actions of all women.

Because Eve was disobedient, the logical conclusion is that all women are disobedient, guileless, weak-willed, prone to temptation and evil, disloyal, untrustworthy, deceitful, seductive, and motivated in their thoughts and behavior purely by self-interest.

"It's been almost 6,000 years since Adam and Eve allegedly defied God. Their story still has an uncanny influence on gender politics. The image of a woman as an evil temptress persists to this day, and not just in the religious sphere. Eve's story remains lodged in society's subconscious."

Was it all Eve's fault? I beg to differ.

Let's consider the real possibility that Eve was framed for a crime she never committed. Moreover, this is the point I intend to prove. If there was a curse placed upon women, I could assure you that a man and not a God placed it upon her. The curse of Eve has male chauvinist, patriarchal bias written all over it. While the accounts may be historical, in nature, it is certainly far from divine. I believe the patriarch stole the earth from the matriarchs. A coup d'etat is a sudden and illegal overthrow of a government. Does this not have the same familiar method of operation as "imperialism," does it not resemble overthrows instigated by small groups of men? When in history have we ever heard of women invading a land and setting up government?

Historical evidence on matriarchy is overwhelming. Women once ruled the earth, not by force, not with the sword, but by the wisdom endowed in their genetic code — the one that men fear so much. The reason I can say with great confidence that feminine energies ruled the planet is simple; by the process of elimination there was no one else. When we unravel the DNA evidence, all we find is mitochondrial Eve, no Adam, not one Y-chromosome dating anywhere close to the 200,000 year mark. There was no Adam because there were no men, apart from the feminine; I believe the man existed as consciousness inside of the woman in the form of potential and later came to be a distinct entity through hypermutation, macho grooming, dress, and gender role classification.

There are unique qualities and abilities endowed with femininity. When women are near each other, they form strong bonds to the point of even synchronizing their menstrual cycles. Interestingly, menstrual cycles are the earliest calendars from which the Julian and Gregorian calendars were born.

The feminine was a living calendar, in perfect alignment with her environment, and the earth was an enchanted forest synchronized with her touch and times of the month. She determined the quantity of food needed by her family because she was the original gatherer. Human-

ity thrived under her position of gatherer and farmer. As the feminine energies joined hands and danced in a circle beneath the full moon, magical things happened. Their ovulations occurred at the time of the full moon. Biological cycles, as well as dreams and emotions, guided the planets. Specifically, the moon and tides interacted with the electromagnetic fields of the earthly celestial bodies, subsequently affecting our world. Feminine touch ruled the world.

Planting food according to the phase of the moon is a centuries-old tradition carried on by ancient cultures all over the world. It is a fact that the moon has a strong effect on our planet and its inhabitants. Its gravitational pull guides the oceanic tides as well as our inner cycles. Plants are no different, as with the sea and our bodies, the pull of the moon affects the planet's water content.

Long ago, people lived harmoniously by the cycle of the sun, moon, and the seasons, and the feminine energies were one with all creation. At that time the feminine was revered as the chief agent of life. This power intimidated most men the same way that it intimidates most men today to have women in a position of authority. So, as a result, men took over. They invaded her kingdom, made her a slave, and then slowly yet methodically they turned the planet into their own personal man cave using phallic symbols as a symbol of their conquest. Here is where the framing came in.

No woman can escape being identified with Eve, or Jezebel, the whore, or slut. Her fate, sealed by God himself, and her role are cemented into scripture for eternity. The law included limits and controls on the feminine energies. As the good book says, "A woman is not to teach or to exercise authority over men, but she is to keep silent. For Adam was formed first, then Eve. Adam was not the one deceived; the woman who was deceived became a sinner. But women will be kept safe through childbirth if they continue in faith, love, and holiness with propriety."

As the legend says, "Eve blindsided humanity down a cursed path of misery due to her disobedience." Acting with total disregard for human life, after being fully warned by God himself (In the day you eat of this tree you will die!), she ate the fruit anyway, and she enticed her husband to join. When their sins were exposed, the man blamed the woman, and woman blamed a snake. Either way, together through their actions, they inadvertently opened Pandora's Box of pain and suffering. God cursed the couple to live in affliction and suffering. "Thorns and thistles you will eat for the rest of your lives." This is the pronouncement for their sins.

We, the offspring of this notorious couple, have been paying the price ever since."

(1Timothy 2:12-14)

The early Christian theologian "Tertullian" (c. 155/160-220 BC) reminded women that they share Eve's "ignominy" of original sin and that they are the odium because they brought about the fall of the human race.

Both Tertullian, a respected Catholic theologian, and Calvin, a leader of the Protestant Reformation, mentioned in the book of Genesis, "Do you not believe that you are (each) an Eve? The sentence of God on this sex of yours lives on even in our times, and so it is necessary that the guilt should live on, also. You are the one who opened the door to the Devil, you are the one who first plucked the fruit of the forbidden tree, you are the first who deserted the divine law; you are the one who persuaded him [Adam] whom the Devil was not strong enough to attack. All too easily, you destroyed the image of God, man. Because of your desert, that is, death, even the Son of God had to die."

(The Apparel of Women, Book I, Chap.1)

Oh, evil woman, full of treason
Forever contrary to reason,

Bringing no man good in any season:
Our children's children to the end of time
Will feel the cruel whiplash of your crime!

It was St. Augustine's philosophy, elevated into absolute doctrine, that only the Church could absolve one of sin. Again, from Achtenberg, "It was an ingenious play of power that kept people chained to the institution with guarantees of forgiveness and eternal life." Women lost on all counts. To maintain the logic that the Church held power, they sustained women's inherent sinfulness. If there had been no evil temptress, no sin would exist, and the promised deliverance would wield no control over the masses.

The doctrine of Original Sin was the legal instrument used by the early churches to subjugate women: the Church, dependent for survival upon an economic power base of unquestioned loyalty, would collapse if people saw women as the gateway to Heaven and not the church. Later, this doctrine became an excuse for torturing and murdering hundreds of thousands of women during the Inquisitions and witch-hunts."

Augustine believed lust was one of the most grievous sins. His view of sexual feelings was extremely radical; he believed that a man's erection was a gateway to sin because a man cannot control it. He blamed women for the internal struggle of men, claiming that they were "stimulating." He wrote into church guidelines a solution for the dilemma was to prevent women from awakening lustful emotions in men Thus he gave instructions that woman, should veil themselves to prevent them from causing a sinful response in the male." Augustine viewed women not only as a threat to men, but also as intellectually and morally inferior: Augustine wrote:

"It is the natural order among people that women serve their husbands and children their parents because the justice of this lies in (the principle that) the lesser serves, the greater . . . This is the natural justice that the weaker brain serve, the stronger. This, therefore, is the evident justice in the relationships between slaves and their masters; that they who excel in reason, excel in power."

Flesh stands for the woman and the spirit for the husband. The serpent represents the enticement to disobey God and the preference for selfish desires. It first approached Eve because as a woman she had less rationality and self-control and was closer to the "lower" or female part of the soul. People equated Adam, on the other hand, with the higher and superior part of the human soul. In fact, his choice to eat the forbidden fruit along with his wife was viewed by Augustine as "An act of kindly companionship, lest she is left alone outside paradise."

In other words, Augustine believed that sin entered the world because man did not exercise proper authority over the woman. In that regard, Augustine saw a noble purpose in rape as a means of keeping women "humble.

For us to understand how Augustine and the host of other forefathers of patriarchy were able to brainwash the masses, which includes many women, into subjugating themselves into chattel slavery, it's important to understand the foundation of laws were ingrained into nearly every aspect of our life, while the woman's matriarchal origin had been kept secret.

The reality we experience has been engineered by the architects of patriarchal rulership. The code of control was cleverly placed into our brains long ago using the day to day language we were given. Words we use innocently and without much thought keep us in a perpetual state of hypnotic submission to male authority. It was among the Canaanites, one of the earliest Patriarch societies, that the concept of a male God who created man in his image was first popularized into written language.

Elohim and El for short refer to the male gods created by patriarchs to replace the earlier Matriarchs as authoritarians. El, served as a prefix or suffix. Words such as Elder, Elites, Elect, Elder, Elevated, Elohim, Temple, Circle, Gospel, Apostle, Disciple, Evangelists, Emmanuel, Gabriel, Bethel, Michael, Angel, Gabriel, etc. The plural term Elohim appears over 2500 times in the Old Testament. Words, such as mandate, manual, manipulation, manifest destiny, etc. All use the prefix man as a subliminal way of cementing male authority into human consciousness. To gain a full and clear understanding of exactly what "he" has done we must go back in time to the original crime scene.

Revisiting the scene of one of the most notorious events the world has ever known is worth the journey, we have to go back: whether truth or fable, the case of Adam and Eve has forever changed the landscape of how the world views women. A once honored goddess, reduced for eternity, to a symbol of sin and disobedience, Eve and all her daughters are immortalized as the patsy's that brought sin and death into the world.

This all was supposed to have gone down in a garden called Eden between 5-6 thousand years ago. This is where, according to the now infamous story, a woman is approached by a serpent and, as the Bible says, "The snake was more clever than all the wild animals the Lord God had made." He goes on to ask, "Did God say you must never eat the fruit of any tree in the garden?"

The woman responded to the serpent, "We may eat fruit from the trees in the garden, but God did say we must not eat fruit from the tree that is in the middle of the garden, and you must not touch it, or you will die." "You will not surely die," the serpent said to the woman.

"For God knows that when you eat of it, your eyes will be opened, and you will be like God, knowing good and evil." When the woman saw that the fruit of the tree was good for food and pleasing to the eye, and also desirable for gaining wisdom, she took some and ate it. She also gave some to her husband, who was with her, and he ate it. And then the Bible goes on to say their eyes were opened, and they realized that they were naked.

According to this Bible record, both Eve and the serpent became the facilitators of the downfall of humankind: the temptress and the devil. This is one of the most famous stories ever told and retold all around the world. What is strikingly peculiar about the entire story is how blatantly it contradicts the secular records and artifacts that predate the Bible book of Genesis by thousands of years. Genesis is believed to have been written by Moses in the wilderness between 1450 — 1410 B.C. However, In Sumeria, around 3,500 B.C., during the last Matriarchal era, the serpent symbolized hope, regeneration and eternal life. In the Sumerian culture, property and the family name were passed through the maternal lineage. Women were equal both politically and socially and held authoritative positions in the temples as Priestesses.

Prior to the transition from Paleolithic to Neolithic times, both women and serpents held reputations as celebrities in Ancient Egypt. Before the arrival of male Gods, the snake goddess culture flourished all through the Middle East, Africa, and parts of Europe. The snake Goddess also symbolized birth and fertility. Birth and fertility are synonymous with sexual desire. Sexual desire is a common bond in the lives of men and women. If there were no desire for sex, then we would not be here.

Sexual desire is a powerful motivation for men. Even to this day, the sexual energy of the feminine is widely used in commerce for the mere fact that sex sells. It has been this way since man's conception. Although Moses writes that it was Eve who was cursed with lust, after her willful disobedience, and as a consequence, "her desire would be for her husband, and he would rule over her." Something tells me that when it came to sex back then, things were much the same as they are today.

When it comes to sex, women always have had the upper hand. It's reasonable to conclude that men, led by their sexual desires, were ruled by women who controlled them via their sexual desires for her. Surely, Moses either intentionally or unintentionally got it twisted. While sexual attraction varied wildly from one person to another during the snake goddess era, only feminine snake goddesses are noted in the historical record and women did not worship their image. By process of elimination, we are left with a man. This particular group of men worshiped woman as Gods in their mythology, and these female Gods were symbolized as sex symbols and represented by serpents. Men were magnetically drawn to the goddess.

Wadjet was worshiped as the Jesus of her era: the key and central goddess of Egypt known to represent fertility, desire, childbirth. She is venerated as the protector of children, and in later years she became the protector of kings. Often depicted as a cobra or as the head of the cobra, Images of Wadjet can be seen rearing from the forehead of the great pharaohs of Egypt. Evidence of her protection is most notable upon the funerary mask of Tutankhamen.

How did Eve and Serpent worship go from Goddess to the sinner? Let's take another look at the stories of Adam and Eve. Who wrote this account? The author accredited with writing Genesis is Moses. Moses is the offspring of Abraham. Abraham is the father of the three dominant religions- Judaism, Christianity, and Islam. Patriarchal religions were the new world order of its day. From these beginnings, a new culture of male domination transitioned male female relations from a partnership of equals to a master-slave relationship.

The King James Version (KJV), New International Version (NIV), and Revised Standard Version (RSV) use the term "rule" to describe Adam's relationship with Eve: "...thy desire shall be to thy husband, and he shall rule over thee." An explosion of male Gods emerged during the same timeline. This is the beginning of the intentional and systematic destruction of the Goddess system. It's reasonable to conclude that the story of Adam and Eve was used successfully to convert a matriarchal world into a patriarchal one.

Chapter Six: THE FEMALE HOLOCAUST

"Burning Times" is the name given to a period during the late Middle Ages and early Modern Era when women were persecuted fiercely throughout Europe under the guise of being witches. The word "witch" first appeared in the writings of the 20th century and derived from the Old English words "Wicca," which had its earliest definition as "Wise Woman" or woman of intuition. Interestingly, a "witch" used to be one of the most respected titles a person could have. Witches carried the knowledge and intuition of the ancient shamans and indigenous medicine women and men, although within the tribes there was no gender bias. The older women enjoyed greater freedom, respect, and longevity; they commonly lived longer than their male counterparts. During the Middle Ages in Europe, life expectancy was forty years, but the wise women, or witches, commonly lived well into their eighties. A great jealousy arose between ambitious men who sort to take for themselves the honor that was being given to the wise women.

Witchcraft became the object of terrorism of its day. The curse against Eve was used as justification for widespread genocide: they needed to erase matriarchy from existence.

The priests began their campaign against women by aiming their attacks at the witches these wise and insightful women who previously

"Inequality is Ungodly."

had enjoyed respect for their intuitive healing powers. Priests portrayed witches as sub-humans, playing on people's superstitions and fears of the unknown, spreading rumors about witches being in alliance with the Devil. During the Middle Ages, thousands of women were therefore tortured and burned in Europe because the priests could. It threatened their egos (the false self that appears real). In fact, the witch-hunts were really an attack on women's intuition rather than witchcraft. Witchcraft was the story that was used to justify their actions against women who stepped out of line. It was male priest matched against female intuition. Indeed, women were labeled as witches if they showed any talent. If the man showed the same kind of capacity, he became a saint. People worshiped him as a miracle-man, and the woman was labeled a witch and burned at stake.

Being accused of having sex with the Devil, was one of many frivolous allegations lodged against innocent women, these individuals were tortured day in, and day out. Eventually, they would give up, seeing no hope — and confessed to actions that never took place. In the end millions of women were burned alive. The torture must have been tremendous; obviously, no one would choose to be burned alive unless its alternative was more painful. The Catholic Church led the Inquisition, and its goal was to seek out heretics and burn them at stake in the name of God. Those who hunted the heretics had a handbook, The *Malleus Maleficarum*, written by Heinrich Kramer and James Sprenger, two Catholic priests, in 1486. This book was a "how-to" guide to hunting and killing heretics and witches. Kramer and Sprenger did not specifically identify all midwives as witches but much of their writing points to such an interpretation. Moreover, their writings, much like Hitler's "Mein Kampf," were specifically designed to incite hatred.

The reputation of having a connection to Satan followed midwives across the Atlantic into colonial New England, but that did not stop them from having an extremely important role in society. Midwives had a chief goal of ensuring a safe delivery and minimizing pain for the mother during childbirth (Sharp 1986). Often, there was only one midwife for a whole village, so she was like the town doctor to that community. Midwives were in high demand. As Tannenbaum stated in her book *A Healer's Calling: Women and Medicine, in Early New England*, "These healers were only targeted because they were women, and if they were men, they would not have been persecuted" (2002). These women were not doing anything different from what was asked of them, except that they were independent and made money.

Indeed, being independent and making money is where the real problems began for the midwives in a male dominated societal context. Their independence is what drew attention to them. Suspicion surrounded any woman in colonial New England, especially if she functioned without a man to depend on, let alone being a woman who was doing well. The women of this time had to maintain a "delicate balance between self-assertion and feminine meekness on a daily basis" (Tannenbaum 2002: xiii-xiv). Midwives who crossed the boundaries of this delicate balance suffered harsh consequences. People punished them for not needing men and for being independent and making money via their profession. In their independence, they "threatened the hierarchies of dominance." The perceived danger in allowing women to exist in such a fashion was that they sparked ideas in the minds of the other women of the colonies. Back in time, where a group of women congregating without a male chaperone was deemed a "coven meeting to worship the Devil," midwives seemed to push the boundaries of acceptability to their maximum. Joel Southern puts it most eloquently when he states, "Her age, social and marital status, autonomy, pagan influences, secret knowledge of herbs, and most importantly, the vilification of her profession as unclean and demeaning served to demonize the midwife."

So, how many women were burned at stake for witchcraft? Some estimates range from between 40,000 and 60,000, while others go as high as 100,000 other sources claim the causalities of the inquisitions were a much higher number in the millions. Whatever the specific number, it is clear that far too many women paid the ultimate price for their intuitive, kind, and healing abilities simply because men saw them as threatening to the status quo.

War Declared on the Clitoris

Early one morning in an African village not far from Nairobi, Kenya, young girls were roused from sleep and taken to a nearby river. Their shivering bodies were plunged into cold waters to arrest the bleeding from their first menstrual cycles; the cold water numbing the genitals is also used as a form of anesthesia.

As a girl shakes and struggles in pain, other women-her aunts and cousins who have also been circumcised hold her down, her legs are held apart, her mouth shut tight so that she cannot scream, run away, or alarm the other unsuspecting children. Soon an elder midwife is ready to perform the surprise circumcisions on the little girls. Her tools vary; she might have a rusty razor, scissors, or a shard of glass. Before the curious child can figure anything out, the midwife slices her clitoris off. Afterward, ashes, herbs, or cow dung are applied to staunch the flow of blood. Female Genital Mutilation: an Overview By Mark Ulyseass.

The following information on (FGM) was provided by **The Desert Rose website:** Female Genital Mutilation is a destructive operation, during which the female genitals are partly or entirely removed or injured with the goals of inhibiting a woman's sexual feelings. Most often, this mutilation is performed before puberty, often on girls between the age of four and eight, but it is increasingly performed on infants who are only a couple of days, weeks or months old (Desert Flower website).

Female Genital Mutilation happens primarily in Africa, particularly in Northeastern, Eastern, and Western Africa. However, it also takes place in the Middle East, in Southeast Asia, and among immigrants in Europe. According to estimates by the World Health Organization (WHO), FGM around the world plagues 150 million women. In Europe, the number of mutilated women and girls threatened by FGM numbers up to 500,000 (Desert Flower website).

FGM may be carried out by professional circumcisers, women who enjoy high status in their societies. But it is also conducted by traditional midwives and occasionally by healers, barbers, or nurses and doctors trained in Western medicine. Often, FGM is carried out without

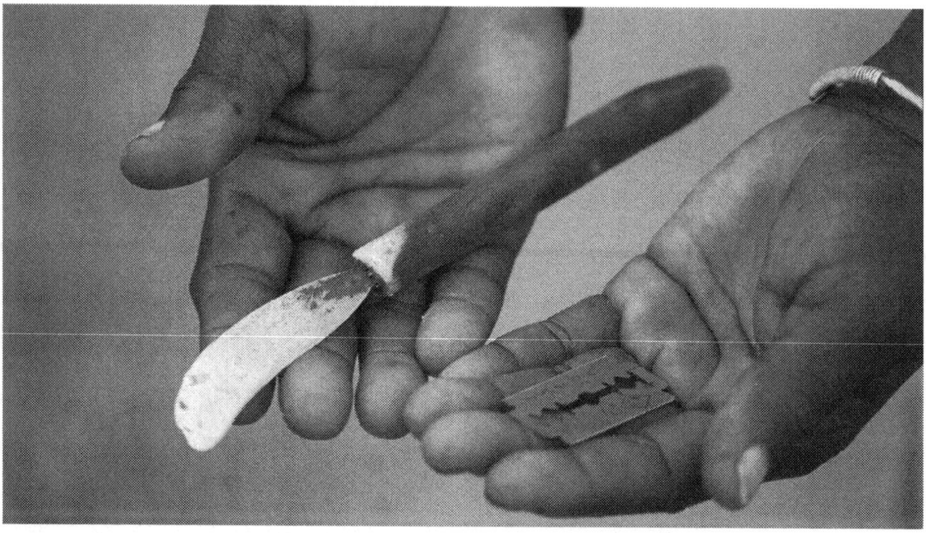

anesthesia and under abysmal hygienic conditions. Among other things, knives, scissors, razor blades, or pieces of broken glass are used as tools (Desert Flower website).

While the United Nations General Assembly unanimously ratified a resolution urging countries to prohibit the practice of female genital mutilation, calling it "irreparable and irreversible abuse," it is still carried out in various societies, including among immigrants to Europe and the United States.

Most types of female genital mutilation involve, among other things, the highly barbaric procedure for removing the clitoris-a preemptive method of controlling women and their sexual desires. The clitoris has one of the highest amounts of sensory nerve endings in the female body and is considered to be her primary source of sexual pleasure. In fact, it is measured that women have an estimated 8,000 sensory nerve endings on their clitoris, whereas men's penises have about 4,000, or half of that. Of further interest is that nearly 75% of women climax through clitoral stimulation only, whereas the remaining 25% may enjoy vaginal orgasms. This means that, when the clitoris is detached, the majority of these women are not able to climax.

Cutting off the clitoris is comparable to removing the head of a man's penis. Imagine what it would be like for a man to have intercourse, much less climax, without the glans of his penis! It would of course never happen, and it is highly unlikely that such a horrific act will ever be perpetrated upon hundreds of thousands of men by other men; or women for that matter. If it were, allied nations of this world would not hesitate to send their best military forces to the rescue. FGM is, however as stated, still happening as a way of controlling female sexuality and boosting the fragile male ego. Men do not usually ask to be castrated or to have the head of their penis cut off. Similarly, these women don't ask for this cruel procedure of having their clitoris removed; they are forced to obey their husbands and their cultures that in some cases make it impossible for a female to be married, facing social exclusion.

In many cultures and regions, female genital mutilation is as normal as male circumcision is in western cultures, yet for vastly different reasons, ranging from reducing sexual desires among budding teenage girls, to the prevention of masturbation (girls again).

Female genital mutilation has sometimes been compared to male circumcision where the foreskin is detached, but it is certainly not similar.

In Type, I FGM, the prepuce (foreskin) and partial or total removal of the clitoris is carried out. In type II, the clitoris and labia are removed. Type III (aka Genital Infibulation) involves removal of the clitoris or Labia Minora, while the Labia Majora are sewn together, leaving a small hole for urine and menstrual blood to exit. The woman, who had Type III FGM will require the scar to be re-opened before intercourse or giving birth, which causes additional, and at times, agonizing pain and future contaminations. In Type IV FGM or Uncategorized genital mutilation, pricking, piercing, cutting or stretching of the clitoris or the labia, or burning and scarring of the genitals likewise ripping off the vaginal opening or the introduction of corrosive compound or medicines into the vagina to tighten it, are widely used.

Instantaneous results of FGM include severe pain and bleeding, shock, difficulties in passing urine, infections, damage to nearest genital tissue, and sometimes death. The procedure can also result in death through serious bleeding leading to hemorrhagic shock, neurogenic shock as a result of pain and anxiety, and overwhelming infection and septicemia (Manfred Nowak, UN Special Rapporteur on torture and other cruel, Inhuman or Degrading Treatment or Punishment).

As a result of the process, nearly all women who have undergone FGM experience pain and bleeding. The event itself is also extremely painful as girls are held down during the procedure. Risk and complications increase based on the kind of FGM and are more severe and prevalent with infibulations (Desert flower website).

"The pain inflicted by FGM does not stop with the initial procedure, but often continues as ongoing torture throughout a woman's life," says Manfred Nowak, UN Special Rapporteur on Torture.

Along with the terrible pain throughout and in the weeks following the cutting, women who have gone through FGM encounter numerous long-lasting results — physical, sexual and psychological, to include Post Traumatic Stress Disorder (PTSD), anxiety, and depression.

Women might also experience persistent pain, chronic pelvic infections, development of cysts, abscesses, and genital ulcers, excessive scar tissue formation, infection of the reproductive system, and diminished sexual enjoyment. Other threats for complications from infibulations are urinary and menstrual disorders, infertility, later surgery (defibrillation and re-infibulation) and mentioned previously, painful sexual intercourse.

The Egyptian feminist Nawal El Saadawi, the writer of "The Hidden Face of Eve: Women in the Arab World," wrote about the frightening experience of her circumcision at the age of six. She also defined her work as a doctor in rural Egypt in the 1950s:

"I very often had to treat young girls who had come to the out-patients clinic bleeding profusely after a circumcision. Many of them close to death because of the inhuman and primitive way in which the operation, savage enough in it, was performed. Others were afflicted with acute or chronic infections from which they sometimes suffered for the rest of their days."

In certain traditions, it is believed that the clitoris will manifest into a penis if it is not detached. As one tribal elder was quoted, girls who were not cut were usually ashamed to swim with their mates and were labeled as hermaphrodites.

According to him, their clitoris grew to the size of their male counterparts' penises. However, for the majority of those traditions which practice FGM, such as in Africa as well as the Middle East, reasons range from it being "a real culture," for religious grounds, rites of passage to womanhood, avoidance of promiscuity among girls, to preservation of virginity, better marriage prospects, and augmentation of male sexual pleasure.

Unfortunately, these harsh traditional practices have already been carried out on over 100 million women alive today. It is evident that education and interventions are required to end this unjust, inhumane, and openly prejudiced traditional practice that deliberately singles out specific parts of the society; particularly people who through particular natural processes have been gifted, or in this case, "cursed" with a clitoris. This singling out is not unlike the torment and enslavement inflicted on people of African ancestry during periods of slavery, for no reason other than being born with a certain amount of pigmentation.

Former supermodel Waris Dirie and author of the book and movie, Desert Flower, surprised the world when she, in an interview in the late 1990's, told the world how she as a five year old suffered from genital mutilation. In her book, Waris recounts the terrible mutilation that took place, being cut with an old razor blade, while being held down by her mother.

"Waris herself nearly died from an infection sustained after the procedure, and later as an adult, she continued to suffer several complications

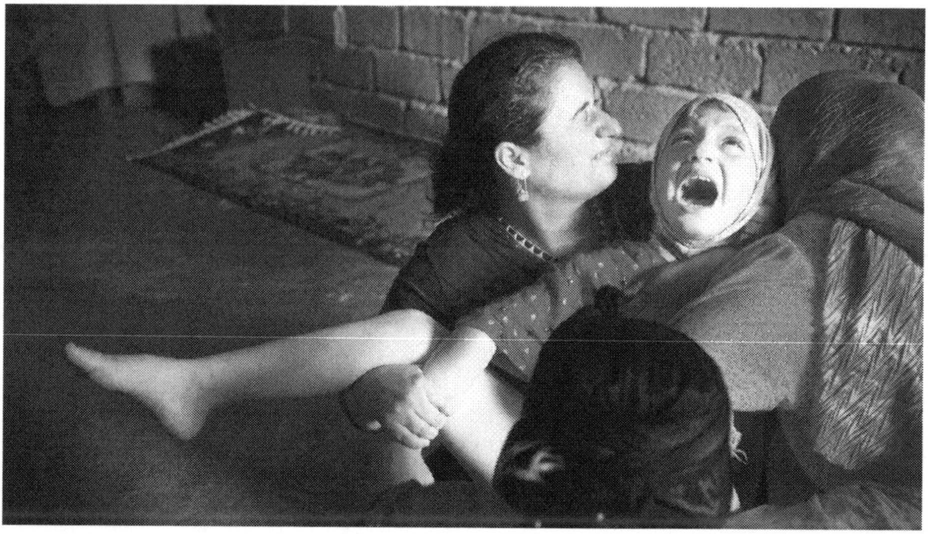

with abdominal pain. When Waris went to see a doctor for her physical conditions, he observed her vaginal opening was just like the size of the bulbous end of a match and stated, "It's a real botch job." One of Waris' sisters died from hemorrhaging going through the same undesirable procedure, and another sister died during childbirth because her vaginal opening was not large enough to accommodate a baby. Waris continued and said that if a young child is not circumcised, she will grow to be an outcast and regarded as at the level of a "whore." Nowadays, Waris is a social activist, and she works tirelessly to save young girls from the victimization of FGM.

Key facts

- Up to 500,000 girls and women living in the European Union are affected or threatened by FGM.
- 75,000 of them live in Great Britain, 65,000 in France, 30,000 in Germany.
- The victims are migrants, whose families took along this practice when they immigrated.

- In spite of FGM in most European countries being either directly or indirectly prohibited, the laws are either incomplete or unenforced. The only country that has ever instituted legal proceedings in connection with Female Genital Mutilation is France.
- Most European countries hardly invest in awareness training and in investigations.
- There are no effective cross-border measures against Female Genital Mutilation. Any efforts — which vary tremendously in their degree — take place within the country borders. FGM is still not considered to be a European problem.
- The victims are usually approached in the health sector and by authorities in an inadequate way; ignorance prevails.
- FGM is in hardly any European country a regular part of the vocational training of doctors, midwives, and social workers.
- No European country explicitly accepts the threat of genital mutilation as a reason for asylum.

To make the point clear, female genital mutilation is an unnatural response to a natural occurrence in nature. It has no health benefits, and it is a violation of women's and young girls' rights. The Creator gave women a clitoris for a reason.

"Remember the ladies, and be more generous and favorable to them than your ancestors. Do not put such unlimited power into the hands of the Husbands. Remember all Men would be tyrants if they could. If particular care and attention are not paid to the Ladies, we are determined to foment a Rebellion, and will not hold ourselves bound by any Laws in which we have no voice, or Representation."

~ Abigail Adams ~

In 1943 Abraham Maslow wrote a theory highly respected in the field of Psychology called the hierarchy of needs simply stated." If a person's basic Physiological requirements for security, food, shelter, and clothing are not met the individual will become psychologically crippled from thriving equally in society."

Chapter Seven: TO FREE THE WORLD, WOMEN MUST BE SET FREE

"I am no bird; and no net ensnares me: I am a free human being with an independent will."

~ *Charlotte Bronte, Jane Eyre* ~

"Transferring control of billions of acres of land to the 3.5 billion women worldwide is a genuine stride toward stabilizing the man-made effects of climate change."

~ *Eric B. Gibson* ~

In 2013, national geographic magazine revealed that 21 million people were evacuated from their homes as a result of flooding caused by climate change. Climate change is one of the supreme challenges of modern times, associated with human polluting of nature's atmospheric range to the point of undermining all living, breathing life on planet Earth.

The Ohio State University has measured that over the last 150 years, 476 billion of tons of carbon have been discharged from farmland soils as a result of improper farming and grazing habits, deforestation, biodiversity loss, accelerated soil erosion, and decrease in organic matter in the ground. Multiple researchers from various fields all point to the human fingerprint on earth as a primary reason in the present state of climate change. Science has simply been unable to find any other cause that may account for the scale of the recent rise in radioactive forcing, or change in the atmosphere due to greenhouse gas emissions and related warming, apart from human interaction.

Historically, women have played an important role in maintaining the hereditary assets of crops. At present, female farmers lead the green revolution and hold a significant role in the cultivation of food all over the world. We can help aid the ecosystem and help reverse global warming by enabling female farmers, and their daughters, larger control of the land currently under the control of reckless corporations. The degree of land being ravaged by desertification is proportionate to the amount of land controlled by these unqualified companies, typically controlled by men. The connection between women and the fertile earth is wonderfully intrinsic and synergistic. The great Mother Earth grows the seed, and for more than 200,000 years, women have been the stewardesses of all the gardens of the world. Together the sower and the grower worked side by side, while men went out hunting.

Women's pre-industrial revolution lifestyle is an environmental and agricultural success story. Historically, there were no environmental security agencies. Female gatherers intuitively understood nature's balance. Practices such as overgrazing by domesticated animals never happened in regions where the tribal women cultivated food. Their gardens were so lush and so incredibly rich in nutrients that there was usually more than enough for everyone as well as animals. In the past, nobody violated an essential law of nature, which states:

"Nothing in nature takes more than it needs; and when something does, it becomes subject to this law and it dies off."

In ancient Egypt, cooperation was epitomized through the concept of Ma'at. This way of life was based upon truth, balance, order, law, morality, and justice. According to Ma'at, living in harmony with nature was essential, as exemplified by the following rule: *I have not laid waste to the land.* Ma'at was represented by the goddess of the same name, a young woman holding a scepter, a symbol of power in one hand, and the ankh, the symbol of eternal life in the other. In her headdress, a feather was the measure of determining whether the souls (residing in the heart) would reach Paradise successfully. Those who made it to Paradise were the ones whose hearts did not weigh more than Maat's feather. In other words, those who lived according to the principles of Maat, reversing the fundamental laws of the universe, such as not taking more than they need.

Human behavior within the past 150 years are a strong indicator that the laws of Maat have been greatly ignored. Everything from the selfish cutting down of the Brazilian Rainforest, to carbon dioxide emissions from motor vehicles are violating the fundamental law of nature mentioned earlier; *taking more than we need.* This is the current system of greed, and destruction. It is literally the architecture and the result of man.

Recently, during a discussion on the popular show TED Talks, environmental scientist Allan Savory admitted that desertification started when the "drum-pounding" natives were expelled from their land by greedy

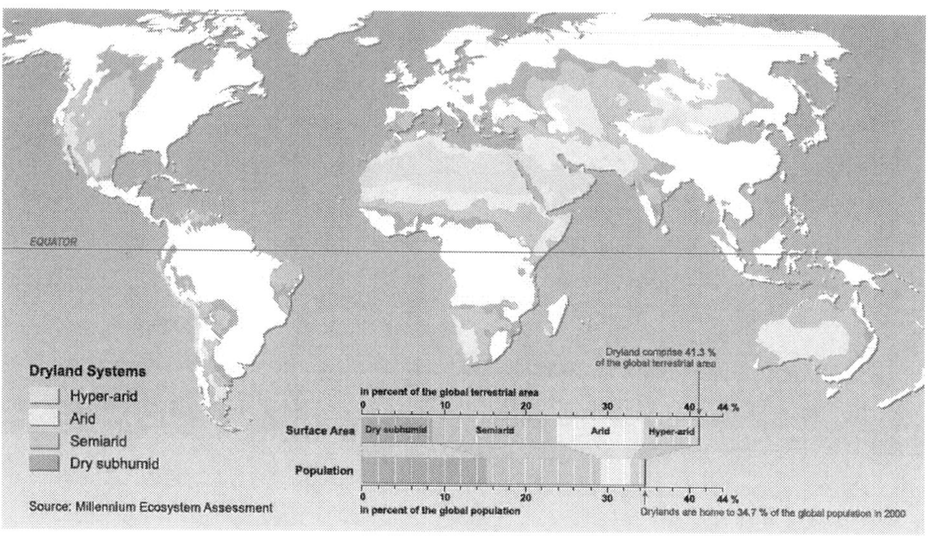

men. Those same "drum-thumping" natives happened to be the women who for so long had been the stewards of the natural gardens of Earth, subsequent to the beginning of time. Women knew their fields, and which types of plants tended to flourish and where to plant. She knew the exact right time at which to pick a fruit; when it was packed with nutrients. But, the men who over time demoted and removed women from these essential and life-giving tasks were unknowing of the consecrated arrangement of life and production with which they were interfering. He was unaware of the importance of never taking more than we need, and the intricate balance existing between every atom of this world. Neither did he comprehend the interconnected web of all life, and that when he destroys one part of this, other parts suffer the consequences. Neither did he understand the full spectrum of his actions, of never rotating his crops, of polluting the waters, and of pumping the plants and soil full of pesticides. Nor did he understand that foods full of chemicals make people sick, contributing to arthritis, leaky gut syndrome, and a whole host of other digestive illnesses and diseases. Or perhaps he did understand but didn't care. Or maybe he just wanted to exert his power and domination over this world, to show how strong, successful, powerful, and profiteering he was.

In a few remote areas of the world, there are still women who live in peace with their patio gardens. One such place is located in the upper Orinoco River in the middle of Venezuela and Brazil. The Yecuana women live according to agrarian practices concentrating on yucca, their staple food. The Yecuana believe that the presence of females enriches the soil and that their harvest is highly dependent upon women's relationship to the earth. In this culture, females not only work the soil, but they also add to it naturally, through their bodily fluids, such as urination and spitting. Interestingly, contributing bodily fluids to the soil is not unlike modern sciences' recent advances that add human protein from saliva and breast milk to rice. Researchers hope their genetically modified rice will help treat diarrhea, a major killer in the Third World. It is quite astonishing that what we deem to be a modern solution to age old nutritional problems has already been practiced for thousands of years, in the ancient cultures, such as the Yecuana.

The expulsion of tribal women from their areas and gardens has made a devastating impact on the earth that has resulted in global warming and desertification. Desertification is the procedure by which the soil is exhausted of its essential nutrients, promoting soil disintegration, which discharges large quantities of unstable and unhealthy carbon into the air, adding to serious environmental changes. This process of desertification is likely one of the biggest problems currently facing mankind. As the Hopi tribe who reside primarily in Northern Arizona, so eloquently said, "This parasitic way of life, or "Powaqqatsi," is a lifestyle that extends the life energy of other creatures to further its own particular way of life." Continuing to live the way we want and exhausting the natural resources from the earth had upset the life cycles of a wide variety of animals, plants, and insects — all of which were doing quite well when women and nature had a symbiotic relationship. In fact, according to the Center for Biological Diversity, dozens of various species are becoming extinct on a daily basis because of the disastrous effects of global warming and habitat loss. Of further concern is that as one species becomes extinct, another one further down the food chain is subsequently affected, exerting a snowball effect causing our delicate ecosystem to fall apart; thus, human suffering and then extinction looms.

Most of the world's food supply was and is created by women. Go as far back in history as you would like, and it will be the same. Women were an integral part of the first original ecosystem, and when we remove or modify this essential delicate framework, then each underlining sub-framework is additionally influenced. This is the law of Cause and Effect. Unfortunately, for many years, scrupulous companies and bribed government officials have continued to exploit the native populations in many parts of the world, causing everything from the death of hundreds of thousands of people (mineral mining in Congo) to serious soil erosion in Sierra Leone making growing anything and living off the land an impossibility.

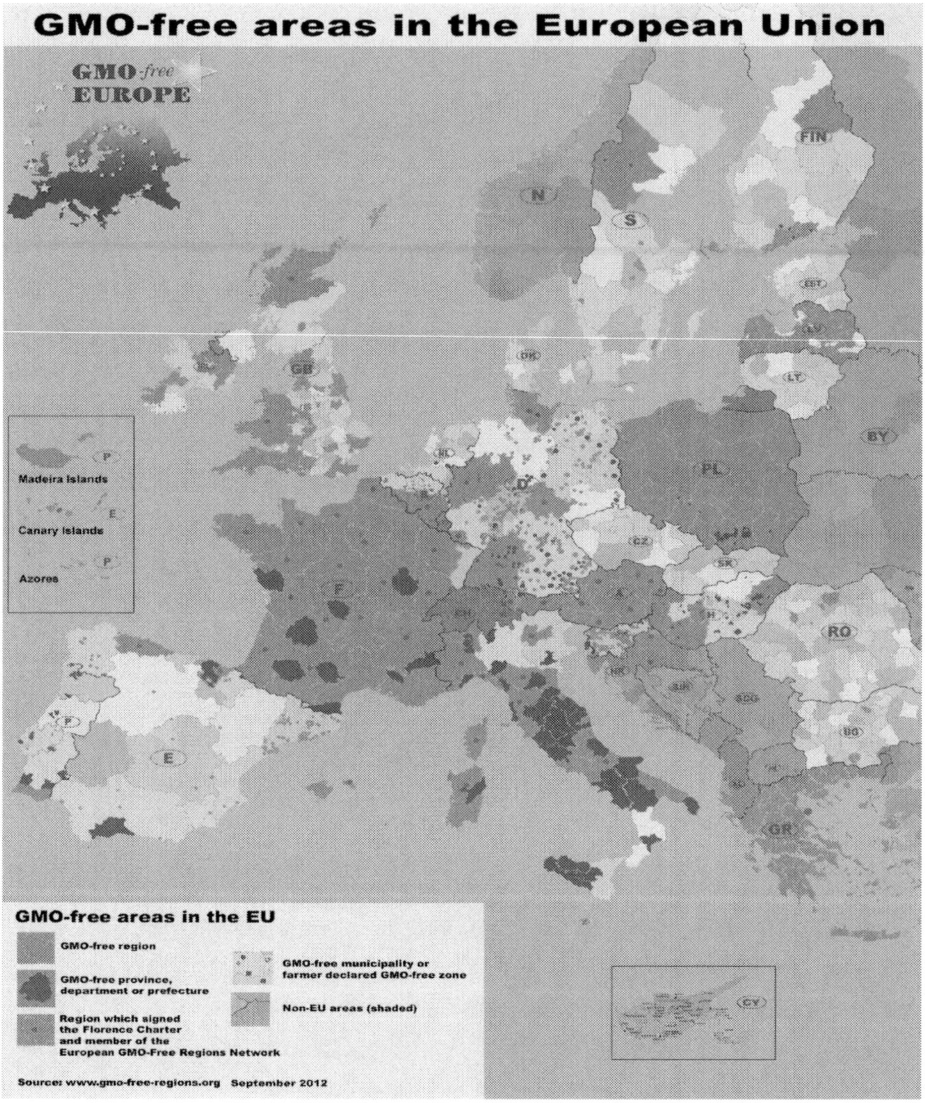

In Brazil, for example, logging companies keen to exploit the rainforest have been accused by human rights organizations of using gunmen to wipe out the Awa, a tribe of just 355 people. However, Survival International, with backing from Colin Firth, is campaigning to stop what the judge presiding over the case has referred to as genocide. In another area of Brazil, over 1,000 gold-miners are now working illegally on

Yanomamo land, transmitting deadly diseases like Malaria and polluting the rivers and forests with mercury. Cattle ranchers are additionally invading and deforesting the eastern fringe of Yanomamo land. Diamond mining can also cause entire ecosystems to collapse, as is seen in the Kono district of eastern Sierra Leone. Here the miners have left behind thousands of abandoned mining pits, causing all of the wildlife to vanish. Topsoil eroded, the land once suitable for farming is now a desolate wasteland.

In sum, when native tribes are forced from their land, there begins a monstrous, cycle that effects everything because everything is interconnected, like a spider web. When we destroy something in one place of the web, it still affects or weakens the whole of this fabric. Consequently, today, the world is confronting a grave issue with the ability to generate enough food, although there are those who say the world has enough food, but it is distributed unequally (greed). Many experts predict widespread famine. Unfortunately, the way in which we try to solve such problems today is centered on risky farming techniques, utilized by corporations such as Monsanto, whose strategy for nourishment creation is extremely disabling to our environment through gene manipulation. Companies such as these have created not only some of the most toxic pesticides that our world has ever seen, genetically modified foods are connected to a multitude of reports of certain diseases becoming more popular, such as Leaky Gut Syndrome. In fact, many European countries have decided to ban GMO foods. It's obvious that the present methods of food production are not working.

The most conceivable way to handle this impending atmospheric devastation is to limit the role of corporations in food production and return the gardens of the world back to women. Give every woman 40 acres of land and the tools to nurse the Earth back to preindustrial revolution condition. The population is estimated to reach approximately 9.6 billion people by the year 2050, and these women would be able to produce enough food to sustain that population.

As it was in the beginning

Ancient Matriarch cultures, much like indigenous tribes, had no governmental style of land ownership. While the manner in which territorial boundaries was established varied from tribe to tribe, many ancient tribes buried their placentas, a traditional practice handed down for generations. This custom allowed tribes to mark their land and establish territorial property via the genetic DNA in the soil. In most ancient matriarch cultures, land was controlled and passed down matrilineally, from Mother to Daughter in this way. Placenta burial is considered a physical and spiritual link to the place of birth. It can be likened to the Western practice of having a deed to show ownership of land. Placenta burial has deep cultural and spiritual significance, as the land is the Earth Mother of the people. The Ibo of Nigeria and Ghana still, to this day, treat the placenta as the twin of the child born and give it full burial rites. In many African cultures, "izan bokui" means "the place where the placenta is buried." The Hopi and Navajo Native Americans of Northern Arizona are two of the oldest continuous settlements in the world. The Hopi have occupied the same land for thousands of years. I was invited to visit this ancient tribe and learn about their customs, an opportunity which, as you can guess, was nothing short of amazing. Many of the elders still teach the traditions of placenta burial. The placenta and umbilical cord are usually buried in a corral and are intended to bind the person to their homeland. The practice of placenta burial is amongst the oldest customs, dating back to the original matriarch times, and the Hopi are one of the oldest matriarchal societies. In the Hopi culture, men are not permitted to own land, but they are allowed to live with a woman, welcomed to cohabitate as long as it is pleasing to both parties. If for any reason, they should decide to part ways or the man should leave, all assets of home and belonging will remain with the woman. This rare glimpse into the ancient world gave me a better understanding of a way of life otherwise foreign to me. The Hopi and Navajo tribes view placenta burial as part of the circle of life. Part of that regeneration of life is to help other things grow or to give back to Mother Earth as she has given to us. It is our reciprocity and connection to the land that has given us life, as well as the ability to survive and flourish.

Chapter Eight: MEN ENDING VIOLENCE AGAINST WOMEN AND GIRLS

"I am still sickened by the refusal of so many to challenge the culture in which harassment and abuse thrive. Men have to do this, as there are too few women. Do nice men want their daughters touched up by creeps?"

~ Suzanne Moore ~

Somayeh and Rana, Acid Attack Victims

According to Amnesty International, brutality against women and girls is one of the world's most pervasive human rights abuses with 1 out of every 3 women experiencing violence during her lifetime. According to their website:

"Living free from violence is a human right, yet millions of women and girls suffer disproportionately from violence both in peace and in war, at the hands of the state, in the home and community. Across the globe, women are beaten, raped, mutilated, and killed with impunity.

Gender-based violence stems from the failure of governments and societies to recognize the human rights of women. It is rooted in a global culture of discrimination which denies women equal rights with men and which legitimizes the appropriation of women's bodies for individual gratification or political ends. Every day, all over the world, women face gender-specific persecution including genital mutilation, sexual slavery, forced prostitution, and domestic violence. At least one out of every three women worldwide has been beaten, coerced into sex, or otherwise abused in her lifetime.

Violence against women feeds off discrimination and serves to reinforce it. When women are abused in custody, raped by armed forces as "spoils of war," or terrorized by violence in the home, unequal power relations between men and women are both manifested and enforced. Violence against women is compounded by discrimination on the grounds of race, ethnicity, sexual identity, social status, class, and age. Such multiple forms of discrimination further restrict women's choices, increase their vulnerability to violence, and make it even harder for women to obtain justice.

States have an obligation to prevent, protect against, and punish violence against women whether perpetrated by private or public actors. States have a responsibility to uphold standards of due diligence and take steps to fulfill their responsibility to protect individuals from human rights abuses. Yet such violence is often ignored and rarely punished. Too often no one is held accountable for these crimes."

The cases of rape in America alone are staggering. According to Rape Abuse and Incest National Network (RAINN) 17.7 million U.S women have been the victims of attempted or completed rape. Women are not the only victims of this scourge, 3% of American men have been exposed to attempted or completed rape as well. According to *Perspectives on Human Sexuality (1999)* by Anne Bolin and Patricia Whelehan, research indicates that in rape-prone societies there is a clear relationship between male dominance and political power. In fact, rape-prone societies were found to glorify strength, power, and violence. In societies such as these, women have very little or no voice in the political sphere or in religious life and are generally regarded as secondary to men.

An emerging group of enlightened men have begun to challenge the deeply rooted, old-fashioned rules of masculinity that embodies the assumption of male superiority.

The idea that women are merely tools to satisfy men's sexual needs, goes back thousands of years. For example, in the fifth century, in Greece, Herodotus of Halicarnassus, asserted that women had to serve as prostitutes, saying:

"By decree, every woman who is native of the country must be once in her life go and sit in the temple of Aphrodite] and surrender herself to an unknown man. [Once a woman has taken her seat she is not permitted to go home until a man has thrown a silver coin in her lap and has taken her outside, to lie with her. As he throws the coin, the man has to say, 'In the name of the goddess Mylitta' — that being the Assyrian name for Aphrodite. [...] When she has lain with him, her duty to the goddess is discharged, and she may go home."

This sordid, twisted history of brutality against women has been going on for too long, and if this cycle of violence is ever to be broken and the predator is to be restored, the first thing that has to change is his mindset and thinking regarding the roles and value of women. This mindset or attitude is the exact element of society that truly weighs upon the spiritual health of culture. A community that rapes its daughters, sisters and mothers is undeniably scraping the bottoms of the barrels of decency and is hardly as civilized as it may proclaim to be. The attitudes in a rape-prone and violent society have to change so drastically, and we must focus on the several points to achieve this goal.

First, in a rape-free society male violence towards women is neither tolerated nor is it viewed as normal and "natural." Second, rape-free societies do not encourage boys to be rough, aggressive, and competitive. Women also have equal power in public decision making and religious rituals and enjoy equal status with men. Thirdly, mocking women's practical judgment or demeaning what is considered "women's work" is not tolerated in this society. In fact, in rape-free societies, both genders see the importance of each other's work and contribution to the family and the community. In short, if we wish to stop violence against women, the view or attitude as a whole that our society has towards females must change.

Casual observers may like to believe that such behaviors and such violence only occur in Third World countries or less "civilized" nations, but the fact remains that the United States ranks in the top three most rape-prone societies in the world, surpassed only by Sweden and South Africa! So, lest we judge others, when it seems that even *our* culture has a lot of thinking and changing to do. This means not only that our society must be rehabilitated, as suggested above, but also that the predator, which is a product of our culture, must be restored before he can again be trusted. To capture a sexual predator, we must act before he acts, disabling the labyrinth of his thoughts at the junction that separates his fantasies from his actions. Castration is the most effective way to do this. Neutered males are more docile and peaceful. However, many cultures view physical castration as cruel and unusual punishment.

Nevertheless, it would be interesting to see if castration could be modified, yet still, retain its level of effectiveness in inducing docility. In other words, would a more accurate identification of the male gender role have the same effects as neutering? If the mental state truly affects the physical, is it possible to accomplish psychological castration, without engaging in the physical practice? And can we achieve this from the same source from which psychopaths derive their power — their prized penis and gender entitlement? If we could convince men that they really are just women who evolved to form penises, perhaps their entire worldview and how they treat women would change? Perhaps this change in their psyche would completely alter the world; ending thousands of years of violence, persecutions, and discrimination against women. You see, anatomically and biologically speaking, a penis is really just an overgrown clitoris (if dihydrotestosterone is added).

The concept of male entitlement began with the idea that having a penis automatically gives men a right to rule and subsequently have their way with women. With this belief also came the entitlement granting permission for men to exert authority over a woman's body (women, as a rule, don't rape men). To reverse this sense of entitlement, it is necessary to enter into the mind of the abuser and introduce a new self-identity, one not based upon the penis. This psychological belief system of entitlement must be redirected into order for a more realistic and egalitarian form of human relations, based on humanist values, to be embraced.

We live in a society so dominated by male thinking that women have to veil their bodies to prevent churning up unwarranted desires from men who are psychologically conditioned by nudity. In fact, rapes of women on college and university campuses are quite commonplace here in this land that we purport to call the "Home of the Free." A patriarchal subconscious structure of reality helps us to continue to treat women as less than men. Every single day we see the signs of unfair treatment and think nothing of it. In fact, we think it is normal; a woman tied to a role as an inferior, like an animal on a leash. This sign of the broken spirit, the wounded duck figuratively, ignites the attack of the culture that looks for weakness; a victim; and his defensiveness and incessant quest for dominance and control fuels his twisted psychological sense of power over his victim. When will it end?

Chapter Nine: DISCRIMINATION AND VIOLENCE

"The violent men too are slaves, slaves to a conduct that was programmed into their subconscious; after they beat the female into submission; they have moments of remorse that last until the next dose of violent, egotistical rage fills their veins with anger, leaving the future repentance helplessly drowning in the bloody catalog of violence recorded in their DNA."

HISTORIANS ONCE BELIEVED that modern humans were more civilized than the indigenous regions they colonialized. Native tribes were viewed as uncivilized. However, in reality just the opposite is true. Modern man is far more dangerous and violent than his ancient counterpart could have ever imagined. Humans have lived in paradise for most of history. Somewhere along their journey out of Africa, they made a drastic detour, most likely at some point during the ice age. The point of detour coincides with the rise of the Patriarchal Era. Perhaps at this pivotal crossroad, the feminine was telling masculinity to make a U-turn, but much like the hyper-dominating men of today's society, he did not listen. Woman universally live in somewhat of a prison planet where they walk around in constant vigilance, tiptoeing through life with caution, the presence of dominating men represents the potential for danger. There is not a mother in the land that will not need at some time in their daughter's life to have that warning talk about man's propensity toward violence. The way a man would fear other men if he was incarcerated is the way women feel every day all over the world.

The scourge of violence that has occupied a glaring dark spot in our human history has a familiar ring and an undeniable method of operation. Statistically speaking, men commit 95% of all violent or aggressive acts in our society and men were culpable at the start of every war in history. It's evident that the idea of race, which expanded to viewing people from a racial perspective, originated from the dominating men who sat down and drafted the architecture and foundation of a race-conscious, color-coded society. This is not to imply that all men are violent; but instead, that the stereotypical dominant male in our society that commits these grave atrocities against humanity deserve further evaluation. To eradicate a pest, we must first understand its origin. Do the way men and women socialize foster violence against women? How did a doctrine of inequality against women first develop? To answer that question, we must go back in history to the time when Greece was a world power and chattel slavery was still in its infancy (338 B.C).

In Plato's Academy, in 338 B.C., the ancient Greek philosopher Aristotle began tutoring and mentoring Alexander the Great. Alexander had, in his short lifetime, conquered most of the world known to man at the time. A young Alexander and his teacher, Aristotle, were pioneers in the flowering science of indoctrination. Many of the ideas of imperialism and colonializing emerged from Alexander and Aristotle, then quickly spread to the territories they conquered. Aristotle traveled the world along with the young Alexander, leaving a path of slavery, pillage, and violence behind him. His conquest ranged from Egypt to India, and in its wake, new ideas which would prove to be detrimental to man emerged.

Slavery became a new issue with the inception of the republic. It was debated whether slavery was natural or conventional. Aristotle asserted that it is the former. His theory of slavery holds that some people are naturally slaves, and the others are naturally masters. It further suggests that anyone who is ruled must be a slave. He marked out the earliest rules for subjugation and placed women at the same status as that of a barbarian. The foundation for categorizing women as slaves was established just 338 years before the Christian era. Within the short course of a few hundred years, Christianity and Judaism would embrace Aristotle's teaching as a doctrine and spread the message of female servitude to every place the Bible was followed. Incidentally, the Bible is probably the most printed and distributed book in the world and it has some interesting perceptions & context in regards to female subjugation.

Leviticus 25:44-46:"*As for your male and female slaves whom you may have: you may buy male and female slaves from among the nations that are around you. You may also buy from among the strangers who sojourn with you and their clans that are with you, who have been born in your land, and they may be your property. You may bequeath them to your sons after you to inherit as a possession forever.* "

Ephesians 5:22-24:" *Wives, submit to your own husbands, as to the Lord. For the husband is the head of the wife even as Christ is the head of the church, his body, and is himself its Savior. Now as the church submits to Christ, so also wives should submit in everything to their husbands.*"

These erroneous doctrines empowered male entitlement and go hand in hand with the cornerstones of rape culture. When an instance of sexual assault makes the news, the method of operation is to blame the victim. Indeed, rape-prone cultures rely on the collective inclination to blame the victim and find excuses for the rapist. Throughout history, violence against women has been accepted and even condoned. More than 2,000 years ago, Roman law gave a man life and death authority over his wife. Similarly, in the 18th century, English common law gave a man permission to discipline his wife and children with a stick or whip no wider than his thumb. This "rule of thumb" prevailed in England and America until the late 19th century. Many feminists claim violence against women is the result of a deeply entrenched patriarchal culture which not only encourages but rewards male domination. In these cultures, men are more likely to use violence to keep their dominant position, and while society claims to abhor violence, it often makes heroes of men who are aggressive, celebrating their perceived masculinity. Indeed, the traditional model of masculinity encourages men to exude an aura of daring and aggression, if not downright sociopathic tendencies.

One of the hallmarks of a sociopath is his inability to connect with and empathize with his victims emotionally. It is exceedingly unfortunate that personality traits such as these are being celebrated in so many cultures around the world. But then again, disconnection and emotional coldness are exactly what enables some men to continue to excuse their violence, their raping of women, wars, fighting, and more. Prior to the advent of modern psychiatry, people prone to violence were said to have "inner demons." Perhaps the inner demon is real violence that was programmed into an individuals' DNA. Interestingly, some scientists say that men born with an extra Y chromosome, or XYY have more violent tendencies than men with their usual set of chromosomes (XY), however, other researchers disagree and say the increased violent tendencies could be explained by socioeconomic variables in the populations studied. In other words, living in a violent area also tends to increase the violence of the inhabitants.

Either way, these rare karyotypes have been found to produce excess levels of testosterone, possibly contributing to aggressive behaviors. Could a discovery such as this help explain the history of aggressive behavior and the feminine holocaust? This is not to say that all violent men have an extra Y chromosome explaining savage behavior. However, it has been argued that perhaps past trauma and behaviors can be transmitted genetically through a stress mechanism.

Behavioral genetics is the discipline concerned with studying the contributions of genetics and environmental influences on behavior. Today, researchers have actually found that a person's experience as a child or teenager can have a profound impact on their future children's lives. Rachel Yehuda, a researcher in the growing field of epigenetics and the intergenerational effects of trauma, and her colleagues have long studied mass trauma survivors and their offspring. Their latest results reveal that descendants of people who survived the Holocaust have different stress hormone profiles than their peers, perhaps predisposing them to anxiety disorders. It is conceivable that results such as these explain why so many men, in general, have tendencies towards violence.

Returning to the European witch hunts that put tens of thousands of women who were accused of being witches to death; the aftereffects of those brutal crimes may still haunt the DNA of the children. The dominating, masculine energy we observe today is the same masculine energy from those times. Put it in a line up, and we have the same perpetrator, and the same method of operation that for millennia has been swinging the paternal ax of hierarchical power. The so-called witches were victims of a McCarthy style character assassination; they were a threat, and the female energies of natural wisdom made the dominating males feel

insecure. Many of these so-called "witches" were wise women who knew about herbs how to heal and nurture people, and how to listen to nature. Others were purely innocent victims of gossip. Yet one of the things they were accused of, amongst many, was gathering and conspiring together.

So, how did these "witches" gather? They gathered in circles, spiral geometric motions symbolizing eternal light and wisdom, dancing naked representing their equality. But to men, these witches and their strange and "other-worldly" dances and their deep and profound understanding of and connection with nature, was a threat. It was this fear of a "magical presence" within the female that over the centuries fueled a deep repression of women that became the pattern the denial of the subtle energies from which the world sprang fort; the integral, the nurturing... the woman.

It is extremely difficult to hold women responsible for the catalog of violence of which dominating males in our society have been the architects. In fact, women were really the original slaves or as John Lennon and Yoko Ono referred to them, as the "nigger of the world, slave of the slave, domesticated into servitude by men for the comfort and pleasure of men." The woman's place was in the home, primarily in the kitchen, and her value was determined by how well she served her owner. This was the unwritten law of the land, a commonly held belief system that we were told came directly from God. Indeed, the Bible says women were to be in subjugation to their husbands, as to the Lord. The penalty for not serving her owner (husband) ranged from beatings to being burned at stake or being hanged. Indeed, the whole marriage ritual of ownership was loosely based upon the procedures used in the breaking of wild horses.

With this imagery in mind, the male's role was to bridle the female (lead the bride) and act as her groom leading her through life by a gold ring. Until recently, the position of women was that of property that could be listed on tax records as an asset to her husband, that he was free to trade her at any whim. This early environment of social injustice became the standard that inspired the further devaluation of human life that we see today.

The Stoning of Soraya M., a recent movie, tells the story of a young woman who was stoned to death after being accused of adultery. Witnesses close to the woman testified that Soraya's husband made the charge of adultery because he wanted to marry a 14 year old girl and could not convince his wife to divorce. Soraya's husband also knew that if she was dead, he would not have to pay child support. He, therefore, began spreading rumors about adultery, which was punishable by death or stoning and her own children were eventually part of the crowd responsible for stoning her to death. Stories such as this are not a remote or unusual case of injustice; in fact, such inequity is profoundly and deeply ingrained in many cultures. This includes the United States of America, a place where kidnappings, rapes, and murders are just another day of hell for the woman experiencing it.

Man was not always prone to acts of savagery. The frequency of violence is still relatively new to the human experience. Historians and archeologists estimate that *Homo sapiens* (thinking man) have been on the earth for about 150,000 years. Most experts also agree that wars and violence did not become prominent until the last 5,200 years. The Farmer Palette, also known as the Great Hierakonpolis Palette, or the Palette of Farmer, is a significant Egyptian archeological find, dating back to the 31st century B.C. It contains some of the earliest hieroglyphic inscriptions ever found and provides one of the first recorded accounts of war and violence between upper and lower portions of Egypt.

Egypt's earliest social conflicts, dating back to 3,200 B.C.E., were mild compared to today's standards. In fact, warfare consisted primarily of using sticks and hand-to-hand combat since more deadly weapons such as swords were not yet developed. Subsequently, evidence of death is not found anywhere in the records of historical battles dating prior to 2,500 B.C. Indeed, the killing was a concept that was still new and was not adopted until after a long period and became ingrained into the human psyche, so much so that today it is an all too common part of life.

However, there was a time when there was no violence, and indigenous tribes around the world lived in male/female gender equality — a testimony to a lost way of peaceful coexistence. Societies such as that still exist and include the Khoisan of Africa and the Koi civilization of Northern Columbia that have no crime or violence. Another one of those peaceful cultures is the Andaman tribe that is believed to have descended from the initial Great Coastal Migration that was the first expansion from Africa which, about 60,000 years ago and brought modern humans to India and Southeast Asia. This tribe is known for exhibiting immense warmth and affection; men and women lying together cuddling, petting, kissing, and hugging for hours, serving as a testimony to who we were before domestication and what we could have potentially become. Interestingly, many women in Western cultures seem to echo the same simple sentiments and basic needs exhibited by the Andaman tribe, when they say, "*can't we just cuddle.*" In contrast to these peaceful cultures with gender equality, respect, and total lack of racial classifications, social conflict usually develops in societies characterized by two things; male domination and imperialism.

Many people may note the story of Adam and Eve and question, saying, "Wait a minute, didn't Cain kill Abel? And weren't their parents the first humans on the earth?" And many may ponder, "Hasn't violence and killing always been here?" The answer is a categorical no! Along the genetic path of our ancestral human journey, murder, violence, and killing did not exist. However, the belief that violence has always been serves as a means of normalizing the menace. Even the Bible recorded accounts of violence that occurred in Eden, contributing to this nor-

malization. It indicates that it may have been just one of many such occurrences, referring to another culture of more recent times. What does this mean? As for the testimony of the origins of the culture (which culture?) to be credible, it would have to come from the original people of the earth. Anything less than that is speculative.

The original humans, based on the human genome project, would be the Khoisan tribe of Africa. The problem for historians and genesis theory believers is that the original people of the area in Africa, previously known as Edo, did not speak a language familiar to most languages spoken around the world today or in the recent past. The DNA of the Khoisans, indicate that our oldest living relatives did *not* have language as we know it today; rather they made clicking sounds like a form of communication. It is therefore highly likely that the Khoisans are the only ones in the world who actually could submit eyewitness testimony to the origins of creation, which would have to be in their written language (rock art), and in their native click language. However, Khoisan history, language, and art do not bear any resemblance to the Adam and Eve story we know so well, nor from the Bible, nor from the account of Cain killingAbel. In fact, Biblical stories do not correlate with the actual behavioral patterns of that period. As such, their credibility is dubious, at best.

To this day, the Khoisans still do not kill each other, and they continue to hold women in a high place of esteem, honor, and respect. Indeed, the popular stories of murder and death recorded in the Bible must have come from a different culture than the Khoisan people of Africa. Indeed, non-domestication of the Khoisans appears to be the prime reason for their non-violent nature, representing the last remnant of natural, unadulterated humans before taming, breeding, genetic modification, schooling, caging, intimidating, coercing, extorting, promising, governing, enslavement, terrorizing, murdering, or the likes of any other violent, deceptive, manipulative techniques or traits of more modern civilized society became "popular."

Having been a student of history for over three decades, I can say without hesitation that the story of Adam and Eve would appear to come from a male dominated era and perspective more closely associated with that of medieval times, and more like the Tudor period, than early creation. Support for this claim can be found in the Book of Genesis chapter 3, the famous story of Adam and Eve, where Adam and Eve disobeyed God by eating of the forbidden fruit, the apple from the "*Tree of Knowledge of Good and Evil.*" There, their eyes opened, and they became aware of their nakedness. Now, here is the disparity, the account in the Genesis story simply does not correlate with the way in which the Khoisans lived, who to this day, walk around naked, or half-naked, without the least bit of inhibition, self-consciousness, or intimidation. Their flesh is merely flesh, and they are not ashamed of their bodies. Accordingly, this idea of the first human couple being so ashamed of their bodies that they had to cover with fig leaves to not anger God does not match with the Khoisan way of life. Nor is it comparable to the culture of death repeatedly mentioned throughout the Bible, along with beheadings, kidnappings, and bloody human sacrifices. In fact, it sounds much more like the male dominated period of the middle ages, known as the "The Dark Ages."

The medieval period was a time where men, women, and children would frequently gather at public executions as a form of raucous social entertainment. In this manner of life, violence was encouraged, glorified, and became habituated into the human psyche. It became the accepted *de facto standard* of normal behavior and by watching this form of violence as entertainment must have done something terrible to them inside, desensitizing them, robbing them of the part of their humanity that cares about other humans. Instead, it inspired violence and acceptance of violence, not just for their generation, similar to the socially accepted way that is watching incredibly violent movies and cartoons affect us today. In fact, famous psychologist Albert Bandura, who conducted the Bobo Doll studies, showed that children who watch adult models act out in violent ways do the same. This violence and cruelty, or the vibration thereof, still echoes through the age like a generational spell that can be felt for many, many years to come, lasting to this day.

Subsequently, the medieval period, a time of bloody carnage, violence, and killing that we read about in the Bible, and still feel the aftereffects from, correlates more closely with Biblical accounts, than any other period in history. It was at this time of the Dark Ages that people used torture to extract information, force confessions, punish suspects, frighten opponents, and satisfy personal hatred. One only has to look at

the violent methods of inducing suffering utilized by Tomas de Torquemada, Grand Inquisitor of Spain, who multiplied the single tribunal at Seville, to a network of two dozen "Holy Offices" during the Spanish Inquisition.

While the Spanish Inquisition was taking place, ancient Greeks and Romans also used torture for interrogation. Until the second century A.D., however, only slaves were tortured. Indeed, by decree, a slave's testimony was admissible only if extracted by torture. The word "torture" comes from the French *torture*, originating from the Latin, "torture," and ultimately deriving from the past participle of "torque," meaning, "to twist." Many characteristically Christian tortures rely on a twisting of the limbs, twisting ligatures, or turning screw mechanisms as the Church discouraged the shedding of blood.

During the 12th Century, aka times of Anarchy, the Norman supporters of the throne practiced torture to extract gold and silver from the peasantry. As the Anglo-Saxon Chronicle puts it, "They hanged them by the thumbs, or by the head, and hung fires on their feet; they put knotted strings about their heads, and wrapped them so that it went to the brain. Some they put in a chest that was short, and narrow, and shallow, and put sharp stones therein, and pressed the man therein, so that they broke all his limbs."

These accounts of brutality and bloodshed match stories similar to both the Bible and the atrocities we hear about today. Unfortunately, however, the culprits to our horrific and violent history always seem to originate from societies dominated by males.

Chapter Ten: IT IS NOT GOOD THAT MEN SHOULD BE ALONE

A wise Bible writer gave the precautionary rule: *It is not good that men should be alone.* When men are left alone or around other dominant men, they are prone to violence. Sporting events that attract men are even known for violence; many times, police or security guards need to be present to prevent men from acting violently.

Women in these similar circumstances also have a degree of herd mentalities, modalities of thinking with the crowd, but these meetings do not usually result in the same mayhem as the boys' club. Women's gatherings usually spawn discussions on a variety of topics about their particular interests, such as health, exercise, perhaps books one has read, wellness, and grooming.

However, it would be exceedingly rare for women to get together either plotting violence or getting into physical fights with either one another or other women in their presence. In fact, most women do not endorse violence and become upset, mortified, and embarrassed when their men engage in physical fights.

When it comes to violent behavior man again is alone. He invented it.

Man's fingerprints can be found at every crime scene as far back as there were crimes. He is the architect and culprit of every war known. The

man is the author of every premeditated thought of violence. He is the inventor of world domination. The woman's hands are free from the blood.

The subjugated cannot be blamed for their own subjugation, and the slaves cannot be expected to share in the sins of their enslaver. Women universally live as inmates of a prison planet where they walk around in constant vigilance, tiptoeing through life with caution; the presence of men represents the potential for danger. There is not a mother in the land that will not need to have that warning talk with their daughters about man's propensity toward violence at some time in that daughter's life.

The way a man would fear other men if he was incarcerated is the way women feel every day all over the world: afraid of being raped.

There are men walking the earth today who believe they are entitled to rape females and that it is natural to blame women.

Economic dependency allows men to mistreat women, to philander, and to take over labor markets and political institutions. Once men have absolute power, they are reluctant to give it up.

Chapter Ten: It is not good that men should be alone

Dominant men are the most dangerous animals on earth. They have killed more of their own kind than any other creature on earth. Collectively, men have also destroyed more ecosystems than any other living being. In addition, man has been responsible for making more species extinct than any other animal and created killer machines and dangerous tools that are not natural. No living being on this earth other than man has created bombs, poisonous chemicals, biotoxins, cars, planes, heavy machinery, and billions of other things that can kill directly or indirectly.

Chapter Eleven: HEALING THE EGO

Before we came to the realization of self, the earth cared for us, and we lived in a childlike state of blissful oblivion. In the absence of selfishness, our needs were few. There was no ego to babysit because there was no consciousness of self. We enjoyed the pure joy and freedom of simply being.

Imagine life without ever having looked in the mirror, and how different our self-perception would be. Without ever seeing, the self leaves self-judgment and subsequent comparison to others. Self-scrutiny and physical self-examination dissipate. If none of us had ever seen ourselves, we would have no comparisons to make based upon appearance. We would have been free from the burden of self. There is a certain amount of liberation from this place in the mind that tells you; you have to be something or somebody, when in fact, you already are somebody. There is nothing you have to *do* to be somebody. Again, you already are. Just like a flower does not have to do anything to be a flower, it already is. As it's been said "a rose by any other name is still a rose."

Have you ever had a momentary lapse in consciousness wherein you forgot you were you? A daydream you awoke from and said, "*Was I daydreaming?*" If so, my next question is: what if you never woke up? There was a time in human consciousness when the dream was all we ever knew.

If we were to go back and recall what the world looked like before we were aware of self, we'd do well to study a child before they see themselves. Before they look in the mirror, they understand nothing of our age of vanity. No need to prove anything, no need to conquer, challenge, compete, be right or be wrong: the only need our forbearers had was the need to be. Have you ever wondered how differently our lives would have unfolded had we not been systematically domesticated like a beast of burden by the fathers of the patriarchal societies? Imagine if you could go back, experience a re-birth, and enjoy an opportunity to view yourself as something more than just skin-encapsulated ego. Suppose that there was something inside which in itself had absolute worth?

When we get lost in our imagination of the past or future, this living moment passes us by, and we do not honor the beauty of now. All we have is now. When we mindfully dwell in the present moment, we become the activity.

The word "Zen" conjures up images of motionless monks lost in deep meditation. This mental image becomes less mysterious when you realize the monks are simply practicing being here now. They just are living in the moment, preoccupied with whatever gets their attention at each moment. The original meaning of Zen is to "blow out or extinguish because of lack of fuel" (*i.e.*, desire). It is sometimes referred to as the state of enlightenment achieved by the Buddha.

The Dhamma Brothers

The documentary, *The Dhamma Brothers*, tells the amazing story of a meditation program implemented at Donaldson Correctional Facility in Alabama, historically one of the most violent prisons in the country. Two Buddhist teachers of Vipassana meditation led a 10-day silent retreat for a volunteer group of inmates. They got up at dawn and meditated for several hours each day. In addition to rigorous daily meditation, the inmate volunteers took vows of silence. For nine of the ten days, they could not speak, read, or watch TV.

During this program, many of the inmates went through an amazing transformation. Daily silence and meditation forced them to confront and accept their existence, including the horrible crimes they had committed. Through this vow of silence, all that was left was their own minds keeping them company, and it became difficult, if not impossible, to ignore whatever thoughts and feelings came up in their consciousness, and escape. Many of them had breakdowns as they felt the full force of their own suffering for the first time — a suffering that was the consequence of failing to be in the moment in their past and of accepting responsibility for what they had done.

At first, the warden was skeptical and thought the prisoners were just acting for the purpose of getting parole. Then, he started noticing major changes in the inmates' behavior. They became less violent and much easier to deal with, with several of them eventually leaving behind their gang affiliations. Even after the program was discontinued, many of the "Dhamma Brothers" continued meditating on their own.

It is hard to doubt a grown man's sincerity when you see tears running down his cheeks. These men were hardened criminals, most of them serving life sentences for murder, who rediscovered perspective and humanity simply by spending focused time with the Buddhist teachers and their own minds, finding their true inner beings.

Spirituality to the Rescue

Many of us grew up in a world where we were conditioned to hide our true feelings and emotions. Keeping our true identity secret can lead us to become antisocial. However, connecting with another human being is what makes us human; we are social creatures and quite naturally and inertly desire a human connection at a biological level. This inward desire for connection mirrors our urge to reconnect with the truth of who we are.

At the heart of spiritual tenets are the suggestions to view yourself in a more honest way. The truth of who we are is the peace we are seeking.

You are as powerful as the resources at your disposal. Mediation is one of those powerful often neglected resources. It is proven to aid in the re-wiring of the brain, thus permitting an individual to learn how to work with urges that have become out of control. By shining a light of awareness upon our urges, we can determine how to respond to issues that in the past would have immediately triggered a knee/jerk response.

In time, we may learn to re-condition our conditioned responses to undesirable behavior. When the urge to engage in socially unacceptable behavior emerges, could the answer be to allow the compulsion to serve us as an ally?

It's not uncommon for people to use activities like sex, drugs or alcohol, or being bound to an unhealthy relationship as a way to avoid painful feelings. The obsessive need for sexual release or the fear of being alone, for example, are simply mistaken expressions of the natural urge we all share to find peace and to return "home."

Kalu Rinpoche of India once said:

"*When an enemy arises in your life, even though you may kill it, another will simply arise, because all arising are simply a manifestation of your own state of consciousness.*"

When dealing with deep wounds give yourself time to learn how to feel emotions you may have conditioned yourself avoid. Feelings are just energy and we have a choice of how that energy is redirected. Those who experience sexual or relationship compulsions, may also suffer from shame due to the society's stigmatization around their behavior. The goal here is to turn that shame into awareness and shift our awareness to compassion. We can finally come to see that our most "shameful" challenges can be held in awareness and tender compassion. From this place, our hearts can hold all suffering

Meditation is plugging back into the vastness of human experience. It is acknowledging that the conscious, declarative mind is only a small slice of the pie. By being attentive to internal triggers, one can learn to recognize and prevent violent outbursts, deviate behavior angry comments, and even self-harm.

Chapter Twelve:
THE HIDDEN ACHIEVEMENTS OF WOMEN

"If women want any rights more than they would get, why don't they just take them, and not be talking about it."

~ *Sojourner Truth* ~

Sojourner Truth

BORN INTO SLAVERY in 1797, Isabella Baum, changed her name to Sojourner Truth. She spent her youth in a New York estate acquired by a Dutch born-American slave master by the name of Colonel Johannes Hardenberg. Like other slaves, she was mistreated. Around 1815, she fell in love with a fellow slave known as Robert, but Robert's master pressured them to dissolve the relationship. Rather than permitting their love to thrive, Robert's master pushed Isabella to marry another slave named Thomas, by whom she had five kids. In 1827, Colonel Johannes Hardenberg failed to honor his promise to free her, so Isabella ran away, and she later notified her master, "I did not try to escape, I walked away in the daylight".

After encountering a spiritual transformation, Isabella became a preacher, and in 1843 she changed her name to Sojourner Truth. Within

this period, she became associated with the expanding antislavery movement At the Women's Rights Convention of 1851, conducted in Akron, Ohio, Sojourner Truth delivered what has been called one of the most prominent abolitionist and women's rights speeches in the history of the United States of America: "Ain't I A Woman?"

Excerpt from Sojourner Truth's 1851 Speech "Ain't I A Woman," Delivered to the Women's Rights Convention in Akron, Ohio:

"Well, children, where there is so much racket there must be something out of kilter. I think that 'twixt the Negroes of the South and the women at the North, all talking about rights, the white men will be in a fix pretty soon. But what is all this here talking about?

"That man over there says that women needed to be helped into carriages and lifted over ditches, and to have the best place everywhere. Nobody ever helps me into carriages, or over mud-puddles, or gives me any best place! And am not I a woman? Look at me! Look at my arm! I have plowed and planted and gathered into barns, and no man could head me! And am not I a woman? I could work as much and eat as much as a man — when I could get it — and bear the lash as well! And am not I a woman? I have borne thirteen children and seen most all sold off to slavery, and when I cried out with my mother's grief, none but Jesus heard me! And am not I a woman?

"Then they talk about this thing in the head; what is this they call it? [Member of audience whispers, "Intellect"] That is it, honey. What does that have to do with women's rights or Negroes' rights? If my cup won't hold, but a pint and yours hold a quart, wouldn't you be mean not to let me have my little half-measure full?

"Then that little man in black there, he says women cannot have as many rights as men, 'cause Christ was not a woman! Where did your Christ come from? Where did your Christ come from? From God and a woman! The man had nothing to do with Him.

"If the first woman God ever made was strong enough to turn the world upside down all alone, these women together ought to be able to turn it back, and get it right side up again! And now they are asking to do it; the men better let them.

"Obliged to you for hearing me. Now old Sojourner has got nothing more to say."

Harriet Tubman, born a slave on Maryland's eastern shore, experienced the tough existence of a field hand, such as brutal beatings. In 1849, she fled slavery, departing her husband and family behind to get through. Regardless of a bounty on her head, she returned to the South at least 19 times to guide her family and countless other slaves to liberty through the Underground Railroad. Applying her native intelligence and drawing on her endless courage, she eluded bounty hunting for a reward for

her capture, which finally went as great as $40,000. She never displaced a fugitive or allowed one to turn back.

Harriet Beecher Stowe penned the book, that forever changed America's attitude toward slavery. Harriet wrote the best-selling novel *Uncle Tom's Cabin* considered to be one of the most influential books ever written. The effect that *Uncle Tom's Cabin* had on the country back then was so powerful that President Lincoln, upon meeting Stowe, is reported to have said, "You're the little lady who started this great war. She has also been called the woman who ended slavery, her book was more powerful than the sword. While living in Cincinnati, Stowe met numerous fugitive slaves and traveled to Kentucky where she experienced the brutality of slavery first-hand. Harriet Beecher Stowe introduced the horrors of slavery to large numbers of Americans and became the object of violent hatred throughout the South. Stowe has said that she had a vision during a church service, which inspired her to write the book. The success of Uncle Tom's cabin (300,000 copies) aided in opening the door for woman to have a role in public affairs.

Josephine Baker

Born Freda Josephine McDonald, she survived the race riots of 1917 by running away from home, at thirteen years of age, Josephine, who had frequently been fond of dancing, left her home to find a better life as a performer.

Arriving in Harlem, New York, a teenage Josephine Baker broke into show business as a vaudeville dancer; Josephine rapidly drew attention and positive feedbacks for her dancing expertise, enthusiasm, and comedic skills. But even in the Negro community, as it was called at the time Josephine could not get away from what was called the paper bag test." The entertainment industry of that time period would not hire anybody darker than a paper bag. Harlem, like most places in the country, was color struck. Josephine had to brighten up her skin with lemon juice and skin-lightening makeup just to get work. Josephine wanted more from life. Later, in her memoir, she would write:

"*The Eiffel Tower looked very different from the Statue of Liberty. However, did that matter? What was the good of having the statue without the liberty, the freedom to go where one chose if one was held back by one's color? "No, I preferred the Eiffel Tower, which made no promises.*"

In October of 1925, Josephine Baker decided to relocate to Paris France, where she quickly gained popularity in the local dance clubs. Life was better for Baker in France; she was allowed to pursue her dreams without having to bleach her skin. Her distinctive personality and skills got attention. The people of France appreciated her rare, exotic, sensual nature. These were the Roaring Twenties, and Paris high society couldn't get enough of Josephine Baker. By the mid-1930s Josephine was an extremely wealthy woman. She invested lavishly in a rundown mansion located in the heart of France, les Midlands where Baker would implement her concept of a "Rainbow Tribe" — the adoption of children of different races and ethnicities." Josephine never forgot her humble beginnings. Her vision was that all children could experience the liberty and liberation she encountered in France.

Baker's Rainbow Tribe was essentially a happy and positive experience loaded with mystery and wonder. Josephine's children traveled the world, meeting royalty and dignitaries calling people like Fidel Castro "uncle" when they were introduced to him in Cuba, and participating in the funeral of Robert Kennedy, who was a close friend of the family.

Women's Experiences Matter

In the shadows of Dr. Martin Luther King's renowned "I have a dream speech, Josephine Baker also delivered an effective speech on March in Washington. She opened by revealing her experiences of battling for survival in the South and chasing her dreams in a segregated America. She said,

"And as I proceed to do the things I did, and to say the stuff I mentioned, they began to battle me …and they whip me with their pens, that is much worse when I was a child, and they burned me out of my home, I was frightened, and I ran away."

These initial events had a profound effect on the way in which Josephine led her life.

Like a lot of women at the transform of the century, Josephine Baker was silenced. While the Civil Rights activity was centered on liberty for all citizens. The plight of women, particularly those of color was virtually neglected.

The inadequate dignity and respect Josephine accepted, irrespective of her achievements, were just as bitter as public efforts to dehumanize her. Baker recalled her return trip on a cruise ship when a white actress failed to have dinner with her. "An essential star was to sit with me for dinner, and at the final moment I discovered she didn't aspire to eat with a colored woman."

Baker acknowledged "being a woman was not just about parenting, it is simply about being known as a human being and having the flexibility to access coffee, dinner, and companionship when and where one chooses. An innovative world demands a clear dream, not just the lack of injustice. Josephine detailed the massive freedom she experienced residing abroad in France:

"I could go to any restaurant I desired to, and I could drink water anywhere I needed to, and I didn't have to visit a colored toilet either, and I have to inform you it was

excellent, and I got used to it, and I loved it, and I wasn't fearful anymore that someone would shout at me."

Like most African Americans, Baker thought another America was feasible, but a new, narrative was needed. Like Dr. Martin Luther King, Jr., she had a vision of being free from anxiety which allowed her to go after her wishes and joyfulness on similar footing. She said, "I was excited, and because I was happy I had some victory, and you know that, too." It was tremendously fitting that a woman could talk about love and happiness on the other side of justice and liberty. Women were not frequent at the lead of the Civil Rights Movement but remained undeniably undoubtedly necessary to its momentum. Reminders of life's joys beyond the wrestle itself were important to strengthen long-term progress. Black women engaged in political activities while working outside the home and supervising family needs inside the home. Beyond the struggle, functioning and in the maintenance of the home life, happiness required to be a goal. Through her work, she exemplified how civil rights are intersectional and vital to the future of the nation.

"You must attend a school, and you must learn to secure yourself. And you must understand how to protect yourself with the pen, and not the gun. Then you can reply them, and I can tell you — and I don't want it to sound corny — but friends, the pen is indeed mightier than the sword," Baker said.

Mo Asumang

Most people, including "men" would be fearful to challenge a member of the Ku Klux Klan to discuss racism, but one filmmaker has created it, her mission to perform it. Mo Asumang, daughter of a black Ghanaian father and a white German mother, decided to take racism head on. In her documentary "The Aryans," Asumang visits Germany to speak to Neo-Nazis and America to bravely walk among Klan associates. "Intolerance stems from ignorance." Says Asmang. And she believes one approach to coach members of these groups is to make them confront a person they hate only. They do not communicate with blacks. Though Asumang persists in acquiring mixed reactions, her existence alone is robustly sufficient to make a great impact for some. If nothing else, these Neo-Nazis and KKK members are, at the minimum, forced to put a pleasant face to an otherwise imagined dream of a biracial person. "I think it completely confuses them, So I take a position there, maybe I feel happy at them, and because it's a human reaction, you want to smile back. So I observe them attempting to hold down the smile, and that's something very impressive."

Milena Einstein

1875–1948 — She died alone and penniless. Nevertheless, some scholars say this little-known woman contributed significantly to the Theory of Relativity.

"*How happy I will be when the two of us together will have brought our work on the relative motion to a victorious conclusion.*"

A young Albert Einstein composed these words to his first wife Milena shortly before publishing the Theory of Relativity. The launch of letters like this one has scholars debating over Milena's engagement to relativity. They met at Zurich's renowned Swiss Polytechnic School. Milena was the only female in the class and only the fifth in the school's record. The daughter of a prosperous Serbian family, Milena excelled at physics and math and was committed to her studies until she met Albert Einstein. The two outstanding scientists fell in love. They lived and worked collectively. But more excited about their unique work than in their classes, both failed their concluding exams. Einstein did well the second attempt but Milena, who had become pregnant, failed hers once more. Later they married and had two extra children, but Milena mainly concentrated her effort on Albert's career. Some scholars think Milena wrote the math for the Theory of Relativity; others say she fixed Einstein's math, and still others claim she was even more deeply included. The paper outlining the theory is authorized with a hyphenated name Einstein-Marty, the Hungarian type of her maiden name Marci.

Albert Einstein had left his wife and children before his work was publicized and never admitted his first wife or her work. However, he did provide Milena with all of the Nobel Prize money. But the money failed to last long. Milena was ill, and she was left looking after their mentally ill son. Einstein went on to great acclaim, but he never again created physics equivalent to the work he did while married to his first wife and collaborator, Milena Marci.

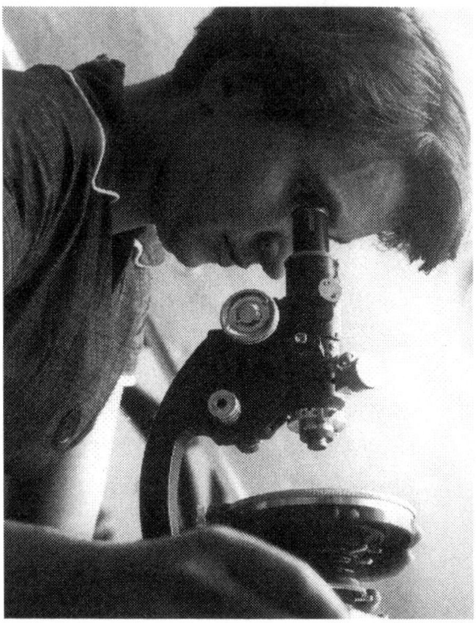

Rosalind Franklin

It is claimed that James Watson and Francis Crick invented the dual helix shape of the DNA. But in reality, they built their work on one of their peers at King's College in London. Rosalind Franklin was an x-ray diffraction specialist whose images of DNA proteins in earlier 1950s exposed a helix shape. It was not until they discovered Franklin's work that Watson and Crick commenced hunting for the long, braided twist that emerged as DNA's double helix shape. Her work was presented to competitors without her authorization who then took the credit.

Why was Franklin not honored for her efforts? Countless have argued that her early death barred her from getting the popularity she deserved since Nobel Prizes can only go to living individuals. Others have proposed something a little more sinister. Nevertheless, James Watson, Francis Crick, and Maurice Wilkins picked up a Nobel Prize for the double-helix style of DNA in 1962, four years after Franklin's pass on at age 37 from ovarian cancer. In 1962, James Watson (b. 1928), Francis Crick (1916–2004), and Maurice Wilkins (1916–2004) collectively obtained the Nobel Prize in physiology or medicine for their 1953 persistence of the structure of deoxyribonucleic acid (DNA). Due to her untimely death from ovarian cancer and since only three scientists can share the Nobel Prize, Wilkins's colleague Rosalind Franklin was not respected.

As I flick through the pages of history, it's hard for me not to notice the role women have played in advancing our society and making ours a better world, while and still forced to live in the shadows of male authority. In 1958 while America was still coming to grip with inequality and discrimination. A quiet woman" Mildred Loving, a mother and housewife, living in Bowling Green, Virginia decided to challenge the State of Virginia's anti-interracial-marriage law. During the times of Jim Crow segregation, Richard and Mildred Loving were arrested, found guilty of falling in love and marrying.

They were thrown in jail on their honeymoon and forbidden to live together as man and wife in rural Virginia. Mildred and Richard had

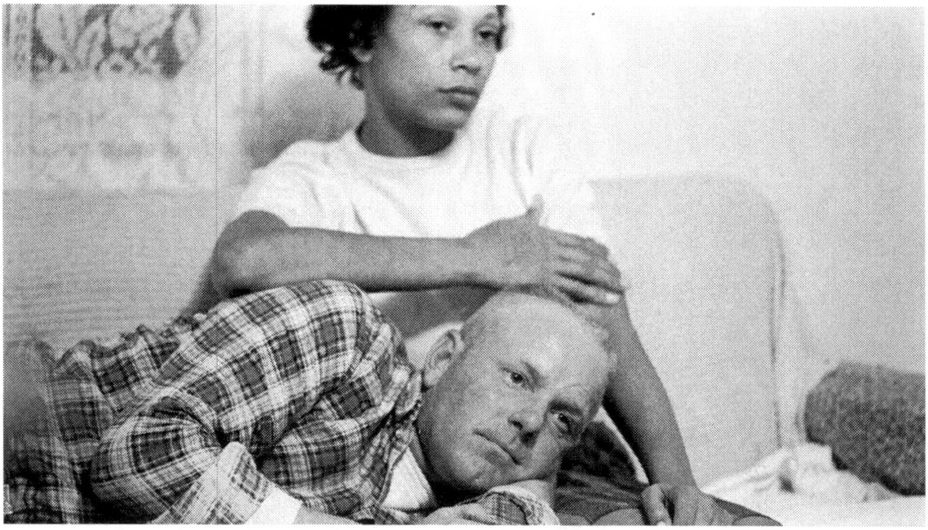

Richard and Mildred Loving

known each other for most of their lives. Their families lived about seven miles from one another in rural Central Point, Virginia. Heartbroken but still very much in love, Mildred Loving decided to write a letter to the then attorney general, Bobby Kennedy. Bobby Kennedy referred the couple to A.C.L.U. civil rights attorney named, Bernie Cohen. Cohen filed the motion challenging the law forbidding interracial marriages right up to the Supreme Court. When asked, "Is there anything you would like for me tell say to them?" In addition, by them meaning the Supreme Court Justice of the United States. Richard Loving, a simple man, who worked as a bricklayer said, "Yes, Yes. Tell the Court I love my wife and it is just not fair that I cannot live with her in Virginia."

The Lovings' ultimately won their case, and anti-miscegenation laws were found unconstitutional. With that, marriage segregation ended In the United States in 1967. In later years, Mildred Loving was quoted as saying 'Not a day goes by that I don't think of Richard and our love, and how much it meant to me to have that freedom to marry the person precious to me, even if others thought he was the 'wrong kind of person' for me to marry. I believe all Americans, no matter their race, no matter their sex, no matter their sexual orientation, should have that same freedom to marry."

Before electronic computers, there were human computers. Katherine Johnson is an American physicist, space scientist, and mathematician, who made fundamental contributions to the United States' aeronautics and space programs Ms. Johnson is one of the original computers who was used to verify the accuracy of digital computers. She also calculated the trajectory for the Apollo space flight.

Katherine Johnson was awarded the Presidential Medal of Freedom in 2015.

Chapter Thirteen:
MY MOM IS MY HERO

My Mother, Shirley E. Gibson

MY MOTHER WAS a home improvement enthusiast years before it became fashionable. Second only, to her passion for art. My mother was a confident woman who did not allow herself to be intimidated by patriarchal authority. Long before the arrival of Home Depot, Lowes, or Dixie-land, my mom was one of the first women to step into the all-male club of the construction world.

A homemaker and mother of five children, Mom was definitely a renaissance woman. Still a head turner, even with her construction boots and work belt, mother became quite the sensation of our middle class Hollis, Queens, neighborhood, she was known as the woman who could build anything. Mother always had a project going, either building something or fixing something around the house. She was quite the spectacle, strolling through the aisles of the neighborhood sawmills sporting blue jeans and construction boots, men often looked at her as if she was a Martian from another planet. She was used to the stern looks of disbelief. The old world was changing; men with unfettered machismo were scratching their heads, trying to adapt to a massive paradigm shift. Women were venturing out of the kitchen into their sacred abode of hammers, nail, levels, and files. I actually felt sorry for them; with my mom! They had no idea who they were dealing with. One day at the Lumber Yard, where mother was strolling down the aisles, old man Johnson growled at her with his raspy smoker's voice:

"Can I help you, lady?" Johnson shouted out with His big white owl cigar dangling from one side of his mouth, as he spoke to mother from the other side of his mouth, head shaking side to side. It was the mid-1960s, and the men of the sawmill had never seen anything like my mom before. Namely a woman who knew what she was talking about.

"Excuse me, sir; do you stock the old 2x4x8 and 1/2-inch lath?" she politely said with her sweetest telephone voice. The old proprietor snapped back with his grouchy cigar smokers' voice. "Those are 2x4s right there in front of you lady. If it were a snake it woulda' bit ya,'" he mumbled against the ambient background noise of chuckles from his cronies who had gathered to-watch the show at the back of the store.

My mom was never shy for words, but was always respectful.

"No sir, actually those are the new style 2x4s. I am interested in the old style. How they ever got away with calling an inch and a half by three-and-a-half-inch piece of wood a 2x4, I'll never figure out!" She pressed, "Well, either way, I need the old size if you carry them. If not, it is okay. I will make do with the new size 2x4s. That's why I asked "you" for the 1/2-inch lath just in case I had to take a new style and modify them with 1/2 shims. Oh, and by the way, those are 10 footers not 8's. If it were a snake, well, I really do need eight-footers." The cigars almost dropped from old man Johnson's mouth. He was speechless, and his face turned beet red. A great hush fell over the whole lumberyard that August afternoon in 1964 against the ambient noise of old man Johnson's cronies snickering in the background. On this day my mother planted a seed for woman's liberation and equality. The little girl from Bayonne, New

Jersey is one of the unsung heroes of the woman's movement and an example for women today. Mother learned her trade through the mere love and passion for the trade.

She was self-taught; she got just as much joy from asking questions as she did from doing the actual work. Always questioning anyone who even remotely knew anything about construction, she loved to pick brains and sucked up the knowledge from anyone she met. She taught herself construction by asking questions. In her interactions with others, it was almost as if she was conducting an interview. Staring deeply into a person's eyes, my mother would make the person she was speaking with feel like what they were saying was the most fascinating thing she had ever heard. Like she was discussing some top secret information. In almost whisper tone mother would say "So you're saying by mixing plaster of Paris into the cement mix I can speed up the curing time. Fascinating!"

I've never met anyone as passionate about building as my mom. She would spend hours at the hardware stores, talking to men about anything from stud walls to plumbing repairs and installations. My mother was also a sculptor and a painter. When she would complete one of her masterpiece's, she would take a step back and just stare, scanning every detail of her work to see if it matched her high standards of excellence. She would get into the "zone" and work in silence for hours, often through the wee hours of the morning, as she sculpted or painted. Michelangelo once said that he did not carve anything; he simply released the beautiful that existed within. This magical, artistic manner of thinking springs from the imagination and leads to the ability to nurture new concepts and new thoughts; and to instinctively comprehend and understand things without having been formally taught. This is the only way we can understand a person like my mother. In my estimation, the artist is the heart of the world. My mother operated in this world of artistic freedom. She raised us to be the same way. On social issues mother taught us treat all people with dignity and respect.

Mother would often pick up homeless people from the street and bring them to our home. She gave them the opportunity to bathe and eat a home-cooked meal while she asked them questions about their lives, making them remember who they really were. Before ending the visit, she would ask them to look at themselves in the mirror, cleaned up, and in some of my father's old clothing. They were imbued with a newfound sense of self-respect. In return, she would simply ask them to promise that they would try to do something with their lives. She had this unique, sensitive knack for making everyone she met feel like the most important person in the world and that they could become a better person because it was already inside them.

In fact, Mom used to say, "We're all like cakes in the oven, some of us just aren't done yet, and some of us are just the product of bad recipes. Hating other people does not change the person. In fact, hate might even be the ingredient that found its way into the original recipe!"

Chapter Fourteen: NEW HORIZONS

IN HER FAMOUS poem, *Still, I Rise*, well renowned poet, actress, dancer, singer, and author, Maya Angelou writes:

You may write me down in history with your bitter, twisted lies,
You may tread me in the very dirt, but still, like dust, I'll rise.
Does my sassiness upset you?
Why are you beset with gloom?
'Cause I walk like I've got oil wells pumping in my living room.
Just like moons and like suns, with the certainty of tides, just like hopes springing high,
Still, I'll rise.
Did you want to see me broken? Bowed head and lowered eyes? Shoulders are falling down like teardrops.
Weakened by my soulful cries.
Does my haughtiness offend you?
Don't you take it awful hard?
'Cause I laugh like I've got gold mines.
Digging in my own back yard.
You may shoot me with your words,
You may cut me with your eyes,
You may kill me with your hatefulness,
But still, like air,
I'll rise.

Does my sexiness upset you?
Does it come as a surprise that I dance like I've got diamonds at the meeting of my thighs?
Out of the huts of history's shame
I rise
Up from the past that's rooted in pain
I rise
I'm a black ocean, leaping and wide,
Welling and swelling I bear in the tide.
Leaving behind nights of terror and fear
I rise into a daybreak that's wondrously clear
I rise bringing the gifts that my ancestors gave,
I am the dream and the hope of the slave.
I rise
I rise
I rise.

A house divided against itself cannot stand and women divided amongst themselves cannot overcome. One of the many consequences of being a member of an oppressed social group is the propensity for the victim to assist their persecutor in oppressing them. It is a natural inclination for anyone placed in a situation where they have to fight tooth and nail for survival, to develop a girl-eat-girl attitude. Patriarchy is a social structure allowing men a monopoly of power while relegating women to a status of subordination. Within the dynamics of this social hierarchy, no matter what a woman does in her life, no matter how hard she toils, how much education she acquires or how rich she becomes, she is not considered an equal member of society.

In the early years of American history, women were discouraged from pursuing higher education because it was considered unfeminine for a woman to be educated. Women who advanced their education were considered "unsexed." Over the last few centuries, women's positions and opportunities in the educational sphere have improved dramatically.

Since 1982, more bachelors, masters, and doctoral degrees have been earned by a woman than men.

Despite the advancement women have made over the last decades, there still exists a counter product tendency for women to cause division among themselves. Fighting over non-essential matters such as a dress, career opportunities or even men! This lack of unity hinders the power of synergy, and synergy is a woman's best friend. Energy works through cooperation. Real power is generated in cooperative endeavors which far exceed the capabilities of any individual. Synergy is a way in which the Universal Mind rewards loving relationships, especially those which are in purposeful service to the greater whole. Gender inequality has long been the Gordian knot of society's woes. To change the future, we must do something different. It's a law of physics. Things in motion will remain in motion till met with a force of equal or greater value. We know economic power is the driving force of gender inequality. Continent by continent, men earn more money than women. Financial Independence for every woman is imperative because a woman's greatest asset should not be her looks. The remedy for solving any persistent problem is "thinking outside the box; the impossible dream must be dreamt for it to have the opportunity to come to fruition. To this end I encourage women the world over to demand financial equality. Imagine women worldwide receiving a paycheck every month to aid in the emancipation of the feminine. We give billions of dollars to poor and undeveloped countries every year. Few if any of those dollars reach the pockets of women. If every woman received compensation designed to grant them independence, poverty could end almost overnight.

This approach to ending poverty and boosting the economy is being implemented in Finland. Finland is planning to issue a check for $876 to every citizen, every month. The concept is called basic income, and the Finnish government is getting closer to finalizing its implementation this month.

The concept of basic income is not new, Dr. Martin Luther King petitioned the United States government for this model of wealth redistribution during the poor people's campaign of 1968. Experts agree nothing ends poverty faster than money. A female based infrastructure is imperative to this reality. Each year women spend trillions of dollars on cosmetic's, breast augmentation, apparel, hair, and nails, etc. so they can attract a man for financial security. Meanwhile, at the end of the day, women own less than 1% of world property and control a micro fraction of the trillion dollar industries they impact by their spending. When society is reengineered allowing women greater latitude over their financial endeavors the patriarchal wall of dominance will fall.

Women of the future will likely be the ones who finally dismantle the empires of sexism and racism through the redistribution of wealth. Numerous studies indicate that women tend to be more charitable when they control resources. In fact, research points towards women having higher levels of compassion than men do, and therefore tend to become more generous when it comes to sharing. Such persons will therefore always attempt to create balance, harmony, love, and peace.

Compassion is not limited to women; it is just not generally exercised by men. For men to access this corpus callosum, they must make a conscious effort. When society tells the man they are right due to their gender, they rarely develop high levels of compassion. There is no need to feel whether their actions are right or wrong. The Awakened Woman is not wired in this way. She does not wish to degrade or exploit anyone. Therefore, if the people of this earth are ready to give up war, fear, violence, and the ultimate destruction of the natural world, securing a future for their children, feminine leadership must be allowed to replace patriarchy with peace.

Made in the USA
Columbia, SC
30 March 2020

90132582R00076